Y0-EKS-987

Cumberland County Virginia Historical Inventory

Subject and Owner Indexes

Patti Sue McCrary

HERITAGE BOOKS
2006

WILLOW BEND BOOKS

AN IMPRINT OF HERITAGE BOOKS, INC.

Books, CDs, and more—Worldwide

For our listing of thousands of titles see our website
at
www.HeritageBooks.com

Published 2006 by
HERITAGE BOOKS, INC.
Publishing Division
65 East Main Street
Westminster, Maryland 21157-5026

Copyright © 2006 Patti Sue McCrary

Other Books by the Author:

*Wilson Families in Cumberland County, Virginia
and Woodford County, Kentucky*

All rights reserved. No part of this book may be reproduced or
transmitted in any form or by any means, electronic or mechanical,
including photocopying, recording or by any information storage and
retrieval system without written permission from the author, except for
the inclusion of brief quotations in a review.

International Standard Book Number: **0-7884-4098-5**

Dedicated

to

Julia (Bransford) Cox and James R Cox

Table of Contents

Introduction

Around 1993, Julia (Bransford) and James Cox of Farmville, Virginia, reviewed the WPA (Works Progress Administration) reports and deed indexes in the Cumberland County, Virginia courthouse. They privately printed the results of their research giving the subject/property names in alphabetical order with the owners as listed in the WPA documents, along with some recent ownership names. This 1996 document is available in the Archives at the Library of Virginia in Richmond, *Index. Historical Inventory of Cumberland County: Works Progress Administration*, Accession # 35348.

The original reports are available, scanned, at the Library of Virginia web site (http://www.lva.lib.va.us/ - from that page select Site Index - from that page select Virginia Historical Inventory). The following is stated on that page:

> Virginia Historical Inventory - An online search engine providing interactive access to photographs, maps, and detailed written reports documenting the architectural, cultural, and family histories of thousands of 18th- and 19th- century buildings in communities across Virginia. This collection was originally assembled by the Virginia Writers' Project, part of the depression-era Works Progress Administration. Report, photograph, and map images are available online.

Some of that data is presented in this document in two index sections. The first section is similar to the Cox document, alphabetically by the subject along with the WPA report number of that subject, which would be an old home, church, mill, etc., with a list of owner names. The order of the subjects is changed to give the primary name first, e. g. Old Smith Place is indexed under S instead of O. Date of ownership, if available, and brief, calculated cemetery inscriptions have been added. Based on the research I have done on families in Cumberland County, I have made corrections and added analysis and sources of information documented by will, deed, order book and other references for some subjects. I have also included some property names that were not in the Cumberland County WPA project.

Footnotes are given in the first section using short titles. A full title bibliography is found at the end of the book. Names and dates with no footnote reference come from the original report and should be checked in county records for verification.

The second section gives an alphabetical listing by owner name, date of ownership if available, and subject/property name. Some names refer to connections to the property other than ownership. Some dates refer to the land, or parcels of the tract, and not the structure at the time of the report. Spelling was changed from the Cox document to reflect the original report.

Patti Sue McCrary
P O Box 2953
Gulf Shores AL 36547
251-948-6143
psbeach2001@yahoo.com

Index by Subject

155   Ampthill

before 1788	Harrison, Carter Henry (1726-1794)[1]
after 1788	Harrison, Robert Carter (1765-)[2]
1835	Harrison, Randolph (1769-1839)[3]
1843	Harrison, William B (1800-1870)[4]
1858	Harrison, Col Randolph(1829-1900)[5]
1870	Randall, Mrs Jane (Harrison)[6]
1908	Harrison, Mrs Harriet (Heillman)[7]
1924	Baker, I M
1924	Rogers, J T
1927	Baker, I M
by 1993	Saunders, James & Dale[8]

62   Ashland

before 1830	Edwards, Daniel C
1830	Lee, Joseph D
1849	Woodfin, Elisha Sr
1855	Woodfin, Sarah
after 1855	McGehee, Sarah (Woodfin)
	Ligon, Mrs Anderson (McGehee)
by 1937	Ligon, W V
by 1937	Ligon, C C

---

[1] Stanard, *Genealogies, Virginia Magazine*, 3:710, 746. Will of father, Benjamin Harrison, land at Willises Creek. Land explanation, birth and death dates of Carter Henry Harrison..

[2] Stanard, *Genealogies, Virginia Magazine*, 3:751, 769. Will of father, residence of Robert Carter Harrison after his marriage in 1788.

[3] Stanard, *Genealogies, Virginia Magazine*, 3:771, 780, 787-8. Purchased brother's Ampthill. The inscription of his tombstone at Clifton is in error.

[4] Stanard, *Genealogies, Virginia Magazine*, 3: 802. Birth and death dates, "died at Ampthill".

[5] Stanard, *Genealogies, Virginia Magazine*, 3:804. Birth and death dates, "died at Ampthill".

[6] Stanard, *Genealogies, Virginia Magazine*, 3:804.

[7] Stanard, *Genealogies, Virginia Magazine*, 3:804.

[8] Cox, *WPA index*, 1.

Ashland (cont.)

	by 1937	Ligon, I G

119   **Auburn**

	before 1790	Trent, Alexander (1729-1793)
	1790	Trent, Stephen Woodson[9]
	1852	Talley, Edwin P
	1853	Page, Archibald
	1857	Page, John C
	1876	Gilliam, Edward
	1888	Perkins, Sarah Price (Gilliam)
	1932	Bryan, Maggie
	before 1969	Ownby[10]

186   **Austin Home**

	before 1792	Austin, James
	1792	Austin, William
	1794	Austin, William & Judith (Atkinson)
	1839	Austin, John A & Frances (Meador)
		Hudgins, Robert & wife Narcissus (Austin)
		Hudgins, Henry C & wife Mary (Austin)
		Hudgins, E A & wife Emily
	1882	Bagby, Mrs Lillian
	1882	Hudgins, Marion A

114   **Barter Hill**

	before 1735	Cary, Henry
	1735	Trent, Alexander (1703-1751)[11]
	ca 1751	Trent, Alexander (1729-1793)[12]
	1789	Trent, Alexander (1758-1804)[13]

---

[9] Avant, *Some Southern Colonial Families*, 4:380,749-750 (Cumb. Co Deed Book 6:574, Bible).

[10] Vaughan, *Crucible and Cornerstone*, 54.

[11] Weisiger, *Goochland*, 73 (Deed Book 2:170) Henry Cary to Alexander Trent land "both sides of Willis River".

[12] Avant, *Southern Colonial Families*, 4:371 (Cumb. Co VA Will Book 1:44) Land to son Alexander.

[13] Avant, *Southern Colonial Families*, 4:379 (Cumb. Co VA Will Book 6:556)

(continued...)

Subject   Year   Owner

Barter Hill (cont.)

	ca 1809	Wilson, Matthew & Elizabeth (Trent)[14]
	1816	Wilson, James[15]
	1834	Wilson, Elizabeth (Trent) & children[16]
	1853	Wilson, Goodrich[17]
	1859	Gilliam, Edward
		Gilliam, V A
	1936	Gilliam, Miss Gay
	1993	Dillon, Mildred[18]
Barter Hill - inscription		Wilson, Elizabeth - 1785-1851[19]
Barter Hill - inscription		Wilson, Edward - 1819-1893
Barter Hill - inscription		Gilliam, Miss Gay

100   Bizarre

	before 1781	Randolph family
	1790	Randolph, Richard & Judith[20]
	1796-1810	Randolph, John "Jack"
	1813	Randolph, Judith
	1936	Swift, Mr & Mrs

---

[13] (...continued)
Barter Hill Tract to son Alexander.

[14] McCrary, *Wilson Families ... Correspondence .... 1785-1849*, 12, 143-6.
Matthew married Elizabeth Trent in 1808. 1809 letters state "Matt's lot was Barter
Hill" and "Mat .... married & settled at Barter Hill".

[15] Cumberland Co VA Deed Book 14:66. In this deed, James Wilson buys the part
of Barter Hill allotted to Elizabeth at the death of her father and allows Matthew,
his wife and children, to live there and for Matthew and/or Elizabeth to devise
Barter Hill to their children.

[16] Cumberland Co VA Chancery Order Book 1831-1851: 46. Court certified death
of Matthew Wilson..

[17] Cumberland Co VA Will Book 12:66. Account of sales of estate of Elizabeth
Wilson by legatees through agent Goodrich Wilson.

[18] E-mail 9 Jul 2000 from John Reid of Peculiar MO.

[19] *Cumb. Co VA Hist Bulletin*, 14(1999):6. The burials. The two inscriptions are
from photos taken by John Reid of Peculiar MO in 1993.

[20] Crawford, *Unwise Passions*, 32, 56-60, 110, 112, 207, 217. John "Jack"
Randolph. 1789 marriage of Richard Randolph and Judith Randolph and move to
Bizarre, 1796 death of Richard. Jack left Bizarre and moved to Roanoke
plantation. The house burned, and Judith moved to Farmville.

63   Blanton Home (Old)

before 1873	Matthews & Montague - trustees
1873	Blanton, Thomas W
1904	Armstrong, A B - comr.
1904	Crute, J M
1912	Clairborne, Lula H
1921	Zimmerman, C E

121   Bonbrook

before 1791	Venable, Abraham B[21]
1791	Wilson, Willis
1823	Wilson, William W & Willis[22]
1847	Wilson, William W[23]
1879	Wilson, Henry J & wife Lucy[24]
1887	Wilson, Mrs Lucy (Gay) & Miss Bettie C Gay[25]
1888	Lawford, Thomas W
1903	Davis, R T
before 1992	Watson, Ray[26]

86   Bonbrook Cemetery

1903	Davis, Robert
before 1992	Watson, Ray

Bonbrook Cemetery - inscription   Wilson, John Park - 1790-1871

---

[21] Cumberland Co VA Deed Book 7:91. 1791 Venable 1500 acres on south side of Willis River to Willis Wilson.

[22] Cumberland Co VA Will Book 7:105. 1821/1823 will of Willis Wilson, wife Elizabeth and son-in-law John P Wilson to live together at Bon Brook during her life and at her death the property to be equally divided between his two grandsons, William Willis Wilson and Willis Wilson.

[23] Cumberland Co VA Deed Book 26:438. Willis Wilson sold his undivided moiety of Bonbrook to William W Wilson.

[24] Cumberland Co VA Will Book 13:647, Deed Book 32:281. 1868 will of Wm W Wilson mentions debt to Mendenhall. 1878 suit by Mendenhall settled by 1879 sale of Bon Brook to Henry J Wilson.

[25] Cumberland Co VA Deed Book 35:69. Mrs Lucy H Wilson and Miss Bettie C Gay to Captain Thomas Wright Lawford.

[26] Visit in 1992 with Ray Watson.

Bonbrook Cemetery - inscription   Wilson, Elizabeth Woodson (Trent)
                                       - 1807-1888
Bonbrook Cemetery - inscription   Wilson, Henry J - 1848-1884
Bonbrook Cemetery - inscription   Wilson, Isaac Gibson - 1863-1864
Bonbrook Cemetery - inscription   Harris, John Lovell - 1848-1857
Bonbrook Cemetery - inscription   Harris, Charlotte Anne - 1854-1857
Bonbrook Cemetery - inscription   Harris, Wallace Deane - 1857-1857
Bonbrook Cemetery - inscription   Wilson, Maria Willis (Wilson) -
                                       1793-1818
Bonbrook Cemetery - inscription   Wilson, Willis Park - 1815-1816
Bonbrook Cemetery - inscription   Wilson, Willis - 1758-1822

23   **Booker Cemetery (Old)**
                                       Booker, Edward
                                       Booker, William
                                       Smith, William James
        1899   Smith, George E B
                                       Smith, George E B - relatives
Booker Cemetery (Old) - inscription   Booker, Rev George E - 1828-1899
Booker Cemetery (Old) - inscription   Booker, E Nash - -1868
Booker Cemetery (Old) - inscription   Booker, Fannie Munford -
                                       1884-1904
Booker Cemetery (Old) - inscription   Smith, Rev G E B - 1871-1915

19   **Booker's Mill**
        1785   Smith, Robert
        1785   Booker, Edward
        1811   Gaines, Bernard
        1811   Booker, Bernard
        1819   Jones, Robert
        1819   Hobson, Maurice
        1819   Booker, Anderson
        1819   England, William
        1819   Booker, Edward
        1819   Hobson, Thomas
        1828   Hobson, Maurice L
        1828   Cook, Stephen
        1828   Hobson, Maurice L
        1829   Booker, Richard
        1829   Hobson, Maurice L

    Subject   Year   Owner

134   Bookers Tavern

before 1842	Booker, Edward
1842	Booker, Thomas
1850	Booker, Mrs Thomas
	Booker, Frederick
	Booker, William N
	Upchurch, Mrs Lillie
before 1902	Smith, William R & L L
1902	Meador, John

150   Boston Hill

after 1732	Carrington, George (1711-1785)[27]
1785	Carrington, Mayo (1753-1803)[28]
1803	Carrington, Ann (Adams)[29]
1809	Carrington, Benjamin
	Richardson, Richard - heirs
	Richardson, Susannah - wife
before 1837	Wisdom, Craddock
1839	Mayo, William H
1883	Duncan, W S
1920	Hatcher, M F
1929	Hatcher, R S
Boston Hill - inscription	Wisdom, C died July 12, 1837

36   Briarfield

before 1831	Johns, James
1831	Flippen, James
1859	Johns, Robert T
1859	McGehee, John B
1867	Blanton, Joseph
1867	Grigg, James A
after 1867	Grigg, Sarah R
1937	Grigg, Sarah R - heirs

---

[27] Brandow, *NGSQ*, 70:259, 262. George Carrington died and buried at Boston Hill.

[28] Brandow, *NGSQ*, 70:263, 265-6. Mayo Carrington died and buried at Boston Hill.

[29] Brandow, *NGSQ*, 70:265-6 (Cumb. Co. DB 12:101). 1809 Ann (Adams) Carrington sold Boston Hill to Benjamin Carrington.

176   **Broomfield/Steger's Farm**
      before 1796   Mayo, Daniel
      1796   Steger, Thomas H
      1839   Steger, Nancy
      after 1839   Steger, Francis E H
      1901   Cowherd, Thomas E
      1902   Fraser, James H
      1909   Dickey, George S
      1911   Carnes, W W
      1921   Pruden, Addie E (Carnes)
      1921   Ehrhart, Mary (Carnes)
      1921   Funkhouser, Lucy (Carnes)
      1933   Carnes, W Sherman
      1933   Carnes, Everett A

13   **Browns Presbyterian Church**
      before 1774   Brown, Davis
      after 1774   Littleton Parish Vestrymen

198   **Buena Vista Site**
      1845   Crowder, Thomas W
      1863   Crowder, William R
      1869   Wilson, John R
      1869   Wilson, John W
      1872   Palmore, George W
      1891   Morton, R G
      1892   Meador, H J
      1926   Meador, Mrs H J
      1926   Meador, Mrs E R

95   **Burleigh Hall**
      before 1810   Cunningham, Richard
      before 1827   Cunningham, Jane
      1827   Cunningham, Edward
      1829   Hobson, William B
      1834   Foster, Peter B
      1841   Pettus, Hugh M
      1878   Budd, H H
      1892   Morrison, W F
      1895   Flippen, Mrs Alice (Morrison)
      1903   Ehrlich, Emil

Subject	Year	Owner

Burleigh Hall (cont.)

	1912	Henderson, W F
	1920	Furr, J M
	1935	Godsey, A E Jr

109   Ca Ira Mill

	before 1795	Keeling, George
	1795	Deane, James
	1795	Deane, Francis
	1795	Deane, Thomas
	1806	Thornton, William M
	1806	Carrington, Edward
	1836	Armstead, James A
	1836	McAshan, William L
	1842	Armstead, Anderson
	1850	Matthews, George
	1850	Sims, Edward
	1871	Woodson, B B
	1871	Palmore, Mr
	1906	Dowdy, R J
	1921	Harvey, C C

164   Cartersville Presbyterian Church

Cartersville Presbyterian Church congregation
(pastors, elders and members named in report)

49   Cedar Bluff/Scott Place

	1828	Colley, William Jr
	1832	Colley, William W
	1843	Colley, Mrs Lenora
		Fitzgerald, Nace
	1880	Wilson, Fanny P
	1901	Scott, George
	1936	Scott, Thomas P

175   Cedar Grove/Bryant Place

	before 1799	Bryant, Isaac
	1799	Bryant, James
		Bryant, Silas
		Bryant, A J, W C, Edward, Silas, Willie
		Oliver, Bettie - Bryant/Oliver, heirs

Cedar Grove/Bryant Place (cont.)

	Davis, Rebecca - Bryant/Oliver, heirs
	Oliver, James - Bryant/Oliver, heirs
	Porter, Ada - Bryant/Oliver, heirs
1901	Oliver, W Edgar
1901	Stratton, Milton M
1936	Jones, P R
after 1936	Tyson, A L

183   Cedar Plains

before 1810	Baltimore, Christopher
1810	Montague, William
1827	Carrington, Benjamin
1838	Carrington, Mayo B & Mary Ann[30]
1838	Carrington, James S & Ann M
1838	Hartsook, Daniel & Elizabeth
1838	Powell, Nathaniel & Sophonisba
1838	Fitzpatrick, Thomas & Mary Ann
1838	Carrington, William
1838	Booker, George
1838	Booker, Samuel
1853	Flanagan, Madison F
1900	Flanagan, James Montague
1924	Flanagan, Madison
1924	Flanagan, Plummer
1924	Davis, Kate
1924	Flanagan, Robert

126   Center Presbyterian Church

before 1847	Hobson, Samuel & Maria
1847	Hobson, James - trustee
1847	Parrish, Valentine - trustee
1847	Trent, William A - trustee
1847	Page, William N - trustee
1847	Jones, Powhatan - trustee
1847	Wilson, John P - trustee
1847	Wilson, William W - trustee

---

[30] Brown, *Cabells and Their Kin*, 296. Death of Benjamin Carrington.

45   **Cherry Grove/Thweatt**

before 1810	Thweatt, Archibald
1810	Eppes, John W
1815	Baker, Jerman
1819	Wilson, Daniel A
1819	Hughes, John
1821	Hughes, Edward
1886	Blanton, Eliza D
	Blanton, Eliza D - heirs
1913	Smith, J Weldon
1919	Bates, John B

54   **Cherry Grove/Sanderson Home**

before 1855	Holman, John
1855	Holman, William
1855	Walden, John E
1918	Holman, Nathan G
1918	Sanderson, Fannie A
1937	Sanderson, Ollie

16   **Chow Chow /Phillips Home**

ca 1832	Phillips, Peter
1851	Phillips, Elizabeth (widow)
1854	Ransom, William
	Palmore, George W
	Power, Thomas
1907	Shepherd, J C
1907	Flippen, O G
1912	Brown, A T
1934	Easterly, D E

31   **Clare Farm/PowersPlace**

before 1840	Palmore, Charles S
1840	Powers, Thomas M
1869	Powers, Spencer B
1904	Powers, T Hyde
1906	Woodson, B B
1906	Smith, William M
1906	Thorbus, C T
1906	Thrawn, Carl
1914	Smith, Dr J W

Clare Farm/PowersPlace (cont.)

Year	Owner
1918	Garnett, George King
1919	Smith, William M
1919	Smith, J Weldon
1920	Wood, John Phillip
1923	Smith, William M
1923	Smith, J W
1925	Meinhard, Amelia M
1925	Smith, Dr J W
by 1937	Smith, Judge William

Clay Bank [31]

Year	Owner
before 1796	Randolph, Thomas[32]
before 1798	Randolph, Isham & Nancy[33]
before 1798	Randolph, Thomas Jr & Mary
1796 & 1798	Wilson, James
1823	Trent, Alexander (1786-1873)[34]
1884	Page, Julia R (Trent) Gray
1910	Gray, Taylor
1912	Spencer, A S
1916	Spencer, W S
by 1991	Bowe, R Patrick & Virginia[35]
Clay Bank - graveyard	Page, Lt Col John C - CSA
Clay Bank - graveyard	Trent, Elizabeth Randolph (1803-1882)
Clay Bank - graveyard	Trent Alexander V (1786-1873)

---

[31] Clay Bank was reported in Buckingham County VA, BU288. It was located in both Buckingham and Cumberland Counties.

[32] McCrary, *Wilson Families ... Correspondence .... 1785-1849*, 68. James Wilson wrote a letter 19 Oct 1796 saying he had recently bought Thomas Randolph's "Clay bank Plantation". This was probably a Buckingham deed.

[33] Cumberland Co VA Deed Book 8:235. Deed dated 19 Oct 1798.

[34] Cumberland Co VA Deed Book 17:175. James Wilson exchanged Clay Bank with his son-in-law Alexander Trent, for Alexander's portion of Barter Hill, which he inherited from his father. The Buckingham Co VA will of Alexander Trent - 4 May 1871 - proved 12 May 1873 - when wife Elizabeth M Trent dies, "Clay Bank to daughter Julia R Gray, wife of J T Gray".

[35] Visit with Virginia Bowe June 1994.

32   Clifton/Meadors

before 1819	Meadors, John
1819	Kirkpatrick, Rev John
1843	Smith, Fred W
1859	Smith, S A
1899	Smith, William M
1907	Smith, Miss Hattie A

149   Clifton/Harrison

after 1745	Harrison, Carter Henry (1726 - 1794)[36]
after 1794	Harrison, Randolph (1769-1839)[37]
after 1859	Harrison, Rev Peyton (1800-1887)[38]
after 1865	Miller, James
ca 1881	Anderson, Elijah G
before 1912	Anderson, Theodore C
1912	Anderson, Wister
before 1993	Metts, Dr & Mrs J C Jr [39]

201   Clifton Cemetery

by 1800	Harrison Family
before 1993	Metts, Dr & Mrs Julian C Jr
Clifton Cemetery - inscription	Harrison, Kitty (Heth) - 1800-1833
Clifton Cemetery - inscription	Harrison, Archibald M-1794-1842[40]
Clifton Cemetery - inscription	Harrison, Mary (Randolph) - 1773-1835
Clifton Cemetery - inscription	Harrison, Carter Henry -1776-1800
Clifton Cemetery - inscription	Harrison, Randolph - 1769-1839[41]
Clifton Cemetery - inscription	Harrison, Randolph - 1798-1844

---

[36] Stanard, *Genealogies, Virginia Magazine*, 3:710, 746. Will of father, Benjamin Harrison, land at Willises Creek. Land explanation, birth and death dates of Carter Henry Harrison.

[37] Stanard, *Genealogies, Virginia Magazine*, 3:771, 780, 787-8. Born at Clifton, bought Clifton from his brother, birth dates and places of his children.

[38] Stanard, *Genealogies, Virginia Magazine*, 3:788,808.

[39] Cox, *WPA index*, 5.

[40] Transcription error. Stanard, *Genealogies, Virginia Magazine*, 3:807. Archibald Morgan Harrison of Carysbrook born 1794, died 1842, age 48, married Kitty Heth.

[41] Transcription error. Stanard, *Genealogies, Virginia Magazine*, 3:787. Randolph Harrison born 1769, died 1839 age 71.

Subject	Year	Owner
Clifton Cemetery - inscription		Randolph, Isham - 1771-1844
Clifton Cemetery - inscription		Harrison, Virginia Randolph - 1834-1850
Clifton Cemetery - inscription		Harrison, Carter H - 1792-1843
Clifton Cemetery - inscription		Harrison, Henningham Carrington (Wills) - 1801-1864[42]
Clifton Cemetery - inscription		Atkinson, Peyton Harrison - 1812-1848
Clifton Cemetery - inscription		Atkinson, Betty Carr (Harrison) - 1826-1847
Clifton Cemetery - inscription		Harrison, Jane Cary (Carr) - 1807-1859
Clifton Cemetery - inscription		Harrison, Peyton - 1800-1887
Clifton Cemetery - inscription		Harrison, Nelson Page - 1855-1855
Clifton Cemetery - inscription		Harrison, Wm Byrd - 1837-1846
Clifton Cemetery - inscription		Harrison, Col Randolph - 1829-1900[43]
Clifton Cemetery - inscription		Harrison, Sally H (Browne) - 1825-1849[44]
Clifton Cemetery - inscription		Harrison, Edward Jacquelin - 1824-1903
Clifton Cemetery - inscription		Harrison, Thomas Randolph - 1791-1833

154   Cobham

	Year	Owner
	ca 1774	Ross, David
		Ross, David
		Ross, William
	ca 1836	Nelson, Judge William
		Nelson, Dr R E
		Nelson, John J
	ca 1937	Nelson, Mrs John J
	1986	Alexander, Emma & Charles IV[45]

---

[42] Stanard, *Genealogies, Virginia Magazine*, 3:808. Maiden name Wills.

[43] Stanard, *Genealogies, Virginia Magazine*, 3:804. Col Randolph Harrison born 1829.

[44] Stanard, *Genealogies, Virginia Magazine*, 3:814. Maiden name Browne.

[45] Cox, *WPA index*, 6.

Subject   Year   Owner

18   Colwell Graveyard
    by 1936 Trent, Albert
 Colwell Graveyard - inscription Colwell, James Madison - 1793

2   Confederate Cemetery -1861
         United Daughters of the Confederacy

192   Corson Home/Coupland's Tavern
before 1807	Cayce, Fleming
1807	Shepard, Samuel
1807	Holeman, John
1814	Yancy, Robert
1814	Yancy, John
1820	Bosher, John C
1822	Coupland, William R
1859	Blake, James C
by 1936	Corson, Charles
1993	Spencer, Sidney Bruce[46]

24   Cottage Grove
1817	Miller, John
1855	Miller, John T
by 1937	Miller, Sam

43   Cottage Grove Cemetery
     Miller, Capt John - no marker
     Miller, Dr John T - no marker
     Miller, Martha Todd - 1785-1850

22   Cumberland Baptist Church/Jenkins Church
ca 1817	Jenkins, Rev Joseph Hull
ca 1817	Church Membership and trustees

81   Cumberland Courthouse [47]
    before 1816 Foster, Peter B

---

[46] Cox, *WPA index*, 6.

[47] The WPA report lists some Cumberland Co VA Order Book page references.

3   **Cumberland Presbyterian Church**
        before 1759   Anderson, Charles
        1759   Church Elders

172   **Dawson Home**
        before 1840   Sims, Col Reuben T
        1840   King, John P
        1843   Austin, James M
                     Dawson, Lewis
        1845   Dawson, Catherine M
        1850   Smith, William E
        1882   Meyers, David
        1892   Dawson, Mrs Ella R

148   **Deanery, The**
        ca 1791   Deane, Francis Browne
        after 1860   Deane, Francis Browne - heirs
        by 1936   Irving, F D

148   **Deanery Cemetery** [48]
                    Irving, F D

Deanery Cemetery - inscription	Deane, Francis Browne Jr - 1796-1868
Deanery Cemetery - inscription	Irving, Paulus A E, M D - 1831-1853
Deanery Cemetery - inscription	Irving, Robert - 1790-1850
Deanery Cemetery - inscription	Deane, Francis B - 1770-1860
Deanery Cemetery - inscription	Frayser, Ellen - 1850-1852
Deanery Cemetery - inscription	Frayser, Dr Benjamin F - 1819-1852
Deanery Cemetery - inscription	Frayser, Elizabeth Deane - 1848-1849
Deanery Cemetery - inscription	Irving, Elizabeth H (Deane) - 1803-1833
Deanery Cemetery - inscription	Deane, Anne H - 1768-1833
Deanery Cemetery - inscription	Irving, Robert T - 1836-1838

---

[48] "Graveyards", *Cumb. Co VA Hist Bulletin*, 1 (1984):40-1. Many more markers located behind the Deanery in Cartersville are transcribed.

Subject	Year	Owner
Deanery Cemetery - inscription		Kirkpatrick, Arianna Deane - 1855-1861
Deanery Cemetery - inscription		Irving, Francis Arianna - 1853-1854
Deanery Cemetery - inscription		Irving, Ann Mildred - 1820-1820
Deanery Cemetery - inscription		Woodson, John - 1716-1793
Deanery Cemetery - inscription		Woodson, John P - 1795-1815
Deanery Cemetery - inscription		Woodson, John - 1765-1832
Deanery Cemetery - inscription		Woodson, Ann S - 1777-1826

30   Dunleith

	before 1840	Palmore, Charles S
	1840	Powers, Thomas M
	before 1892	Powers, S B
	1892	Diggs, Charles D
	1896	Walker, C M
	1896	Shepard, S W

125   Effingham House [49]

	before 1775	Langhorne, Maurice (1721-1791)[50]
	after 1791	Langhorne, William Beverly
	1807	Hobson, Thomas
	ca 1840	Hobson, Samuel
		Foster, Peter
	ca 1867	Haas, Charles
	1867	Robinson, John
	1908	Smith, William M
	1908	Woodson, B B

---

[49] *Gish, "Effingham Tavern", Cumb. Co VA Hist Bulletin,* 13 (1998):13–14. Dr. Gish gives an updated history and lists the tavern-keepers 1747-1842.

[50] McCrary, *Wilson Families ... Correspondence .... 1785-1849,* 59-60. A letter written 10 Mar 1795 mentions the death of Mr Langhorne and the sale of his estate, how the family were "quite worn out keeping the Ordinary at the Court House", the death of Mrs. Langhorne, the family living with Mrs Moulsen who soon died, and some of the guardians of the children. Cumberland Co VA Order Book 1792-1797:12 lists similar guardians. Cumberland Co VA Order Book 1788-1792:59-60. 23 Feb 1789 - "Relative to a house burnt of Maurice Langhorne .... used as a Court house ... to said Langhorne right to any compensation".

Effingham House (cont.)

	1916	Montague, Annie K
	1918	Garrett, R C
	1747	Trigg, William - Tavern-Keeper
	1760	Word, Thomas - Tavern-Keeper
	1774	Carrington, Joseph - Tavern-Keeper
	1777	Gaines, Bernard - Tavern-Keeper
	1780	Fendley, David "at the courthouse" - Tavern-Keeper
	1797	Smith, Robert - Tavern-Keeper
	1789	Langhorne, Maurice - Tavern-Keeper
	1800	Langhorne, William Beverly - Tavern-Keeper
	1802	Hobson, Thomas - Tavern-Keeper
	1817	Eggleston, Richard S - Tavern-Keeper
	1824	Hobson, Maurice Langhorne - Tavern-Keeper
	1829	Foster, Peter B - Tavern-Keeper
	1833	Hobson, William B - Tavern-Keeper
	1837	James, Francis H - Tavern-Keeper
	1842	Palmore, Charles S - Tavern-Keeper

156 Elkora/Walnut Hill

		Carrington, James L (1813-.....)[51]
		Harrison, George F (1821-....)[52]
	1855	Harrison, Major Carter Henry (1831-1861)[53]
	after 1861	Harrison, Major Carter H heirs[54]
	by 1936	Harrison, Mary L (Harrison) Mrs E C

120 Englewood/Horn Quarter

	before 1761	Harrison, Benjamin (....-1761)
	1761	Harrison, Cary
	1798	Scruggs, Edward

---

[51] Brown, *Cabells and Their Kin*, 297. James Lawrence Carrington son of Benjamin.

[52] Stanard, *Genealogies, Virginia Magazine*, 3:807, 813, 814. George Fisher Harrison, son of Carter Henry Harrison and Janetta Fisher.

[53] Stanard, *Genealogies, Virginia Magazine*, 3:807, 813, 815. Brother of George F Carrington.

[54] Stanard, *Genealogies, Virginia Magazine*, 3:815. Children of Carter H Harrison.

Subject	Year	Owner

Englewood/Horn Quarter (cont.)

	1823	Scruggs, Edward L
	1829	Page, Nelson
	1830	Page, William Nelson
	1850	Walton, Anthony A
	1854	Branton, William A
	1863	Lancaster, William
	1867	Lancaster, Fannie V
	1891	Cullen, William T
	1894	Parker, Holland
	1897	Jacques, Susie
	1903	Davis, E R
	1903	Rudd, W T
	1906	Davis, E R
	1913	Belmore, Chris
	before 1919	Davis, E R
	1919	Nuckols, M W
	1922	Federal Land Bank
	after 1922	Emerson Family
	before 1934	Federal Land Bank
	1934	King, R W

116   Farmview

	before 1816	Trent, Edward
	1816	Trent, Alexander
	1823	Trent, Alexander Jr
	1823	Wilson, James
	1831	Fuqua, Joseph & Ann
	1841	Adams, John G
	1920	Franklin, S C
	1928	Franklin, B S & Lee
	1932	Owenby, Pearl
Farmview - inscription		Eliza and Dilcy, faithful servants
Farmview - inscription		Adams, John G - 1799-1852
Farmview - inscription		Adams, Lucy O - 1803-1881

130   Felixville

	1812	Taylor, John D
	1814	Ballew, Charles
	1814	Wallace, William
	1814	Ford, Hezekiah & Co

Felixville (cont.)

Year	Owner
1814	Goodman, Jack
1814	Taylor, William
1814	Wallace, Sam
1814	Ford, Sterling
1814	Harris, Allen H
1814	Frayser, John
1814	Clarke, Francis I
1814	Ford, Newton
1814	Brown, John
1818	Goodman, Zachariah (whole town 1818-1823)
	Federal Land Bank
by 1936	Owenby family of Tennessee
1811	Jeter, Rhodophil - trustee
1811	Jeter, Allen - trustee
1811	Skipwith, William - trustee
1811	Goodman, Norton - trustee
1811	Bransford, Jacob - trustee
1811	Booker, Richard - trustee
1811	Gordon, Thomas - trustee
1811	Bransford, Benjamin - trustee
1811	Colquitt, John - trustee
1811	Powell, William - trustee
1811	Wiley, John - trustee
1811	Booker, Pink - trustee
1811	Farris, Jacob - trustee
1811	Goodman, Zachariah - trustee
1811	Tyree, David - trustee

168   Flippen Home

Year	Owner
before 1832	Johns, Joseph
1832	Flippen, James W
	Flippen, Menville A
	Flippen, James W Jr
by 1936	Flippen, Arthur
by 1936	Flippen, Herman

94   Fork, The

	1782	Page, Major Carter (1759-1825)[55]
	after 1825	Page, Nelson (1801-1850)
	before 1874	Irving, Frances D - wife Lucy Cushing
	1874	Beatty, Francis I
	by 1935	Adams, John S

104   Fork Cemetery

Page Family

Fork Cemetery - inscription	Page, Robert Burwell - 1806-1837
Fork Cemetery - inscription	Page, Lucia Cary (Harrison) - 1809-1842
Fork Cemetery - inscription	Page, Nelson - 1801-1850
Fork Cemetery - inscription	Cushing, Catherine Thornton - 1833-1834
Fork Cemetery - inscription	Dame, George Washington - 1858-1859
Fork Cemetery - inscription	Irving, Robert - 1850-1853
Fork Cemetery - inscription	Meredith, Bettie (Cushing) - 1831-1865
Fork Cemetery - inscription	Irving, Lucy (Cushing) - 1830-1855
Fork Cemetery - inscription	Page, William N Jr - 1841-1861

7   Forkland

	before 1830	Isbell, Lewis - heirs
	1833	Crowder, William B
	1835	Glover, James H
	1835	Glover, Robert B
	1835	Crowder, William B
	1848	Henderson, Robert
	1862	Perkins, Ann J
	1898	Hazelgrove, Joseph W
	by 1937	Hazelgrove, Joseph W - heirs

153   Fork of Willis Church

	before 1856	Daniel, Robert & Louisa
	1856	Carrington, Mayo B - trustee

---

[55] Wall, *Cumb. Co VA Hist Bulletin*, 12 (1997):8. Additional burials are given - Major Carter Page and his wife Lucy.

Fork of Willis Church (cont.)

1856	Goodman, Joseph N - trustee
1856	Flanagan, Madison - trustee
1856	Perkins, Jesse - trustee
1856	Stiger, Francis E P - trustee

80   Foster Graveyard (Old)

before 1813	Anderson, Jesse
1813	Langhorne, Maurice Jr
1831	Foster, Peter B
by 1937	Foster, Peter B - grandchildren
Foster Graveyard (Old) - burial	Foster, Mr & Mrs Peter B Sr
Foster Graveyard (Old) - burial	Foster, Peter B Jr
Foster Graveyard (Old) - burial	Foster, Mr & Mrs John T

42   Foster Place (Old)/Hobson Place

	Thompson, Benjamin
before 1797	Coleman, Gulielmus
1797	Cheshire, Benjamin B
before 1831	Langhorne, Maurice
1831	Foster, Peter B Sr
1872	Foster, Courtney C
	Foster, Peter B Jr
before 1931	Hobson, Rosa V
1931	Foster, Samuel C

191   Frayser's Tavern

	Bransford, Francis[56]
before 1835	Hobson, Epa
1835	Frayser, William A
1841	Hobson, Benjamin
1845	Frayser, William A
	Brazeal Family
before 1932	Whitlock, Jennie (Brazeal)
1932	Goodman, Charlie

---

[56] Cox, *WPA index*, 9.

110   **Glebe, The** [57]

	before 1747	Easeley, William
	1747	Easeley, Wharam & Elizabeth
	1772	Carrington, George - vestryman
	1772	Trent, Alexander - vestryman
	1772	Hatcher, Frederick - vestryman
	1772	Hobson, Adcock - vestryman
	1772	Wright, George - vestryman
	1772	Allen, Samuel - vestryman
	1772	Wilson, Benjamin - vestryman
	1772	Scott, Seymour - vestryman
	1772	Carrington, Joseph - vestryman
	1772	Glen, Nathan - vestryman
	1772	Carrington, George Jr - vestryman
	1772	Langhorne, Maurice - vestryman
	1773	McRae, Rev Christopher - minister, Church of England
	before 1823	Woodson, Miller
	1823	Woodson, Alexander, Tscharner & Miller Jr
	1823	Caldwell, John
	1848	Corson, Mary A
		Corson, William C & Jennie H
	1883	Wilson, Albert
	by 1936	Trent, Albert
Glebe, The - inscription		Talley, James Madison - 1793

83   **Glen Mary**

	before 1846	Perkins et al
	1846	Hubbard, Edmund W
	before 1876	Hubbard, Bolling et al
	1876	Hubbard, Philip A
	1878	Elam, Mary E
	1901	Elam, James B
	before 1926	Carruthers, Lizzie B

---

[57] The Glebe was the land belonging to Littleton Parish of the Church of England. McCrary, *Wilson Families ... Correspondence .... 1785-1849*, 30-1, 201-2. James Wilson letter written 25 Aug 1788 from "Littleton Glebe in Cumberland" and Matthew Wilson letter written 31 Oct 1820, "family of our old reverend & decsd friend Parson McRae".

Glen Mary (cont.)

	1926	Elam, Irving G

160   Glentivar

	before 1723	Randolph, Thomas
	1723	Carter, Robert
	before 1743	Harrison, Benjamin (ca 1695-1745)[58]
		- wife Anne Carter
	1745	Harrison, Carter Henry (1726-1794)
	1790	Harrison, Randolph
	1818	Harrison, Carter Henry
		Harrison, Janetta R
	1845	Harrison, Peyton
	1857	Wood, John T
		Shores, Sally Ann (Wood)
		- Mrs John Francis[59]
		Wood, Watson
	1890	Randolph, Dr John
	1895	Brown, Abram T
	1908	Blunt, Annie E
	1911	Berry, Oscar H
	1930	Sutton, Mrs Hallie (Shores)

133   Goshen

	before 1840	Ford, Hezekiah
	1846	Clarke, Thomas B
		Clarke, Thomas B - heirs
	1894	Clarke, James E
		Clarke, James E - heirs
	1921	Parrish, H T
	1929	Federal Land Bank
	1937	Lamb, J F & Nannie Clee
	1970	Robins, Dr Alexander Spotswood[60]

---

[58] Stanard, *Genealogies, Virginia Magazine*, 3:746. Robert Carter's will - to daughter Anne's second son "to be christened Carter".

[59] Stockman, "Glentivar", *Cumb. Co VA Hist Bulletin*, 2 (1985):43. Daughter of John T Wood, grandmother of 1930 owners. The article gives more recent owners.

[60] Robins, "Goshen", *Cumb. Co VA Hist Bulletin*, 1 (1984):35. Goshen was built
(continued...)

Goshen (cont.)
| | 1983 | McClellan, Dr & Mrs James |

108   **Grace Episcopal Church**
| | 1840 | Grace Episcopal congregation |

187   **Gravel Hill**
	before 1835	Thomas, Joseph
		Thomas, James
	1846	Peasley, Gabriel B
	1855	Stevens, Absolem
	1858	Bryant, Silas S
		Jackson, Benjamin F
	1863	Goodman, Robert T
	1864	Beale, John J
	1865	Flanagan, Madison
	1900	Trice, P J
	1909	Wood, Joshua R

26   **Gray Home**
	before 1847	Hughes, John
	1847	Scott, Thomas
	before 1891	Scott, Thomas - heirs
	1891	Gray, Mrs Ida Scott
	1918	McCrum, J W
	1919	Gilbert, N H
	1921	Addleman, Andrew J
	1928	Addleman, Mrs Andrew J

162   **Greenwood**
		Smith, Henry
		Holman, William
	by 1936	Holman, H S

6   **Guinea Church/Tuggle's Meeting House** [61]
| | before 1824 | Tuggle, Thomas T |

---

[60] (...continued)
in 1840, and owners in 1970 and 1983 are named.

[61] Stanley, *Cumb. Co VA Hist Bulletin*, 1 (1984):30-1.

Guinea Church/Tuggle's Meeting House (cont.)

1824	Ligon, Daniel
1825	Eggleston, Edmund - founder
1825	Miller, John - founder
1825	Allen, Daniel A - founder
1825	Presbyterian membership

47   Guinea Church Cemetery

Guinea Church

Guinea Church Cemetery - inscription	Johnson, Hugh - 1832-1908
Guinea Church Cemetery - inscription	Johnson, Louisa (Henderson) - 1848-1916
Guinea Church Cemetery - inscription	Johnson, Lucy Nelson (Page) - 1852-1895
Guinea Church Cemetery - inscription	Hughes, Martha H - 1831-1908
Guinea Church Cemetery - inscription	Hughes, John Woodfin - 1831-1898
Guinea Church Cemetery - inscription	Hughes, William Blanton - - 1916
Guinea Church Cemetery - inscription	Crawley, Thomas Lilburn - 1916-1917
Guinea Church Cemetery - inscription	Crawley, Maggie Tinsley - 1844-1911
Guinea Church Cemetery - inscription	Crawley, Charles W - 18?5-1890[62]
Guinea Church Cemetery - inscription	Crawley, Hanna Fennell - 1867-1929

41   Guinea Mills

before 1780	Johns, Joseph
before 1780	Johns, Thomas
before 1831	Flippen, James
before 1831	Flippen, James - heirs
before 1859	Johns, Robert T
1859	McGehee, John B
1867	Blanton, Joseph
	Blanton, J J

---

[62] The "?" in the inscription is as reported. Possibly 1835.

Subject	Year	Owner

Guinea Mills (cont.)

	by 1937	Blanton, Joe
Guinea Mills - inscription		Blanton, John R - 1881-1930[63]
Guinea Mills - inscription		Blanton, John James - 1848-1909
Guinea Mills - inscription		Blanton, Laura P - 1854-1924

10   Hendrick Home (Old)

before 1832	Hendricks, Matthew & Frances
1832	Hendricks, David & Eliza
1842	Allen, Benjamin
1889	Allen, James Thomas
by 1936	Allen, James Thomas
1993	Allen, Haynie[64]

17   Hickory Hall

1832	Skipwith, George N
1832	Skipwith, Mary
1832	Hughes, John
1844	Scott, Joel J
1855	Scott, George O
1855	Scott, Thomas W
1856	Womack, Nathan
1925	Womack, Pattie C
1937	Womack, Mary
1937	Snyder, Mrs Sallie
1937	Diggs, Mrs Sterling

196   Hickory Hill/Hard Bargain

before 1848	Jones, John H
1848	Robinson, John B
1896	Robinson, William B
1911	Lancaster, William
1911	Woodson, B B
1915	Leard, Ellsworth

4   High Hill

before 1836	Miller, John & Martha

---

[63] "Graveyards", *Cumb. Co VA Hist Bulletin*, 1 (1984):41.

[64] Cox, *WPA index*, 18.

High Hill (cont.)

Year	Owner
1836	Morton, W S
1870	Blanton, Jas W
1870	Price, Fannie P
1870	Wilson, John W
1870	Berkeley, Ellen
1870	Manson, Polly
1870	Blanton, James W
1873	Crute, J V
1881	Garnett, Mattie
1910	Garnett, John C

73   Holman Place (Old)

Year	Owner
before 1851	Holman, John
1851	Holman, William
	Holman, Nathan G
by 1937	Holman, John

179   Hooper's Rock

Year	Owner
before 1811	Mayo, Joseph
1811	Mayo, George
1813	Mayo, Thomas T
	Mayo family
1845	Trevillian, John M
1846	Jackson, Elisha
1866	Jackson, Elisha, Elvira, & B F
	Peters, Sally
	Brock, Lucy A
	Mosby, Victoria G
1904	Bowles, James Cocke
by 1936	Bowles, James Cocke Jr

21   Hors du Monde

Year	Owner
before 1814	Harrison, Edmund (1764-1828)[65]
1814	Skipwith, William
1823	Robertson, Wyndham
1823	Taylor, Samuel

---

[65] Stanard, *Genealogies, Virginia Magazine*, 3:789,818. This is possibly Edmund Harrison, who married (2) Martha Wayles Skipwith.

Hors du Monde (cont.)

	1823	Robertson, John
	before 1870	Wilson, John W (ca 1796-1870)[66]
	1870	Wilson, John W - daughters
	1870	Berkeley, Ellen (Wilson)
	1875	Womack, Nathan
	1903	Womack, Nathan - widow & children
	1914	Smith, Dr Weldon J
	1914	Brown, A L Jr
	1918	Brown, A L Jr - widow & daughter

152   Hudgins Tavern/Locust Grove

	by 1815	Hudgins, John
		Hudgins, Henry V - executor
	1839	Anderson, Richard I
	1887	Anderson, Wister & Hildreth
		Anderson, Sallie
	1917	Piercy, A N
		Federal Land Bank
	1931	Duncan, P L

159   Irwin's Tavern Site

	before 1833	Irwin, William
	1863	Irwin, Mary B
		Barker, Charles J - heirs
	1896	Barker, Joseph M et al
	1902	Barker, W J
	1911	Parker, Spencer W

137   Jesse Thomas Site

	before 1776	Thomas, Jesse
		Ferris
	by 1936	Sanderson, Mrs C R

203   Jiltic Farm/Booker's Mill

	1895	Daniel, Dr W S
		Crowder, T W
	1911	Smith, Dr J W

---

[66] Cumb Co VA Will Book 13:552. 1870 will of John W Wilson.

Jiltic Farm/Booker's Mill (cont.)
>   1917   Smith, William M
>   1935   Atkins, W T

144   Johnson's Cemetery

Johnson's Cemetery - inscription	Johnson, Martha - 1823-1859
Johnson's Cemetery - inscription	Fraysier, Narcissa M - 1847-1896
Johnson's Cemetery - inscription	Johnson, Mary B - 1808-1864
Johnson's Cemetery - inscription	Johnson, Alexander - 1804-1878

105   Langhorne's Tavern [67]

before 1767	Langhorne, Maurice
1767	Calland, Joseph
1778	Thompson, Josiah
	Thompson, William
1794	Coleman, Gulielmus
1797	Cheshire, Benjamin
1812	Langhorne, Maurice Jr
1819	Richardson, John H & Mary A
1823	Langhorne, Maurice Jr
1831	Foster, Peter B
1834	Watkins, Richard
1911	Brereton, Mrs Ethel (Watkins)
1927	Peters, B A
1932	Horan, Thomas
1936	Federal Land Bank

85   Liberty Hall

before 1831	Langhorne, Maurice & Elizabeth
1831	Foster, Peter B
	Foster, Mrs Peter B
1872	Foster, John T
by 1938	Foster, Thornton & Fannie

35   Locust Grove/Nelson

1822	Nelson, Andrew
1822	Crowder, Thomas W
1825	Miller, John

---

[67] This is apparently the tavern on the south side of the road. See Midway.

Subject	Year	Owner

Locust Grove/Nelson (cont.)

	1825	Crowder, Thomas W
	1851	Crowder, John E
	1889	Walker, E S

50   Locust Grove Cemetery

	before 1825	Miller, John
	1825	Crowder, Thomas Wilson
	1851	Crowder, John E
	1889	Walker, E S
Locust Grove Cemetery - inscription		Wilson, Martha J - 1835-1860
Locust Grove Cemetery - inscription		Garnett, Robert S - 1821-1898
Locust Grove Cemetery - inscription		Garnett, Sara W - 1830-1890
Locust Grove Cemetery - inscription		Garnett John E - 1860-1877
Locust Grove Cemetery - inscription		Crowder, Thomas Wilson - 1795-1855
Locust Grove Cemetery - inscription		Walker, John E - 1888-1906
Locust Grove Cemetery - inscription		Walker, Sallie - 1867-1900

55   Locust Grove/Hendrick Home/Allen Home

	before 1832	Hendrick, Mathew
	1832	Hendrick, David
	1842	Allen, Benjamin A
	1889	Allen, Thomas J

55   Locust Grove Antiques

		Allen, Benjamin A
	by 1937	Allen, Thomas J

202   Locust Grove/Francisco [68]

	ca 1788	Francisco, Peter

135   Locust Grove/Flippen

	1811	Flippen, William
	1867	Sanderson, Jane

---

[68] This house is located in Buckingham Co (BU4) close to Cumberland Co. In the division of the estate of James Anderson, ca 1788, daughter Susannah, wife of Peter Francisco received 60 acres. Reynolds, *Cumberland Co VA Will Books 1 & 2*, 83.

Locust Grove/Flippen (cont.)
                1867   Flippen, Amanda F
                                Sanderson, Fannie & Nannie
                1895   Smith, William Robert
                1908   Phillippi, John

57   **Locust Hill/Palmore**
                1800   Palmore, Joseph L
                1878   Gauldin, Josiah
                1878   Palmore, Charles B
                1897   Palmore, Martha J
                by 1937   Palmore, James Watson
                by 1937   Palmore, Charles B Jr

178   **Locust Hill/Mayo**
                before 1851   Mayo, William
                1851   Mayo, Edward C
                1851   Mayo, William H
                1899   Gary, John A
                1913   Gary, Mildred

157   **McCullough Tombstone**
                1936   Flanagan, R S
        McCullough Tombstone - inscription   McCullough, William's wife -
                                1808-1841

185   **Meador's Store/Old Store**
                1845   Hughes, John & Mary
                1845   Crowder, Thomas W
                1863   Crowder, Harriet
                1863   Crowder, William R
                1872   Palmore, George W
                1891   Morton, R C
                1892   Meador, H J

190   **Melrose**
                before 1859   Carrington, Codrington[69]

---

[69] See Oakland, on which report is stated that Codrington Carrington also owned
"Melrose".

Subject	Year	Owner

Melrose (cont.)

	before 1876	Garret, J Wesley
	before 1876	Gray, Herbert
	1876	Gray, James T
	1903	Winifree, W R
	1908	Arden, John
		Day, George K
	1920	Martin, John M

96   Midway/Langhorne's Home

	before 1812	Cheshire, Benjamin B
	1812	Langhorne, Maurice Jr
	1813	Anderson, Jesse
	1814	Sims, Bernard
	1821	Blanton, John
	1821	Sims, Edward W
	1821	Langhorne, Maurice Jr[70]
	1831	Foster, Peter B
	1834	Watkins, Richard
	1836	Page, William N
	1843	Scruggs, Gutheridge P estate
		Scruggs, Edward P estate
	1843	Palmore, Joseph S
	1848	Wilson, John R
	1851	Miller, John T
	1855	Fuqua, Joseph
	1863	Logan, Lloyd
	1867	Smith, Nannie B
	1867	Smith, Martha C
	1867	Smith, Alice A
	1867	Smith, Anna L
	1879	Watkins, Bennett
	1885	Chappell, Albert
	before 1937	Chappell, Varina E (Mrs Albert)

---

[70] This home is located on the north side of the road, across from Langhorne's Tavern. Maurice Langhorne Jr accumulated land from 1812 to 1821.

8   **Mill Mount**

1778	Skipwith, Henry
1801	Skipwith, William
1806	Baker, German
1806	Eggleston, Edmund
1808	Harrison, Edmund
1880	Woodson, Blake B
1910	Woodson, H D
1910	Woodson, B B
1917	Smith, H P
1925	Woodson, Mrs Lillie P
1925	Federal Land Bank
1935	Payne, Dr Thomas E

51   **Millview**

before 1845	Lee, James D
before 1845	Lee, James D - heirs
1845	Blanton, James M
	Blanton, S J
1904	Badgett, Nannie T
1913	Stibbins, Joseph Jr
by 1937	Bank of South Boston

52   **Millview Cemetery**

Same as Millview - no inscriptions

200   **Minter Site**

about 1800	Minter family
	Page Family

90   **Morningside**

1857	Walton, Dr Richard (1819-1898)[71]
1878	Anderson, Elijah G
	Anderson, daughter m E J Harrison
1922	Harrison, Mrs E J

147   **Morven**

before 1820	Mitchell, Cary

---

[71] *Today and Yesterday*, 288.

Subject	Year	Owner

Morven (cont.)

	Year	Owner
	before 1820	Harrison, Randolph (1769-1839)[72]
	1820	Randolph, William & Jane
	1831	Nash, Abner
	1833	Cunningham, John A
	1837	Harrison, Eliza
	1852	Talley, William C
	1870	Bogert, George W
	after 1871	Bogert, Miss Lilly
	by 1993	Whitlock, George[73]

40   Mountain View/Locust Level

	Year	Owner
	before 1839	Crowder, Thomas W
	1839	Spencer, John
	1839	Spencer, Lion G
	1844	Spencer, Elizabeth W
	1863	Scott, George O
	1863	Logan, Lloyd
	1864	Scott, George O
	1865	McRae, Mrs Emily
	1899	New, Elizabeth R
	1906	McRae, Donald
	1906	McRae, Paul
	1932	Federal Land Bank
	1934	Frank, Rev & Mrs Luther B

Mountain View/Locust Level - inscription	Spencer, John - 1786-1845
Mountain View/Locust Level - inscription	Spencer, William V - 1820-1858
Mountain View/Locust Level - inscription	Spencer, Elizabeth W - 1793-1850
Mountain View/Locust Level - inscription	Spencer, John D - 1810-1844
Mountain View/Locust Level - inscription	Spencer, D H D - 1812-1844

---

[72] Stanard, *Genealogies, Virginia Magazine*, 3:787-8. Elliott, *Marriages, Cumberland Co VA*, 108. William Randolph and Jane Harrison married in 1817.

[73] Cox, *WPA index*, 14.

68   **Mountain View/Meador Place**
    before 1814 Anderson, Jessie
    1814   Russell, Nancy
    1858   Russell, Ann
    1858   Russell, Fannie & Richard
    1881   Meador, Leake S

184   **Mount Airy**
    before 1852 Toler, William & Frances
    1852   Toler, William L
    1874   Fleming, Elizabeth
    1874   Smith, Martha S
    1874   Toler, William B
    1874   Toler, Miller
    1874   Toler, Minnie
    1924   Flippen, W C

174   **Mount Elba**
    before 1837 Shields, Major David
    1837   Shields, Polly C
    1837   Shields, Alfred
    1837   Shields, Judith
    1837   Shields, Mary
    1837   Shields, Henningham
    1837   Shields, Virginia
    1837   Shields, Thomas
    1837   Shields, Joseph
    1854   Shields, Thomas P
    1901   Thurston, T J & C L
    1912   Terrell, A J
  Mount Elba Cemetery - inscription Shields, Major David - 1768-1837
  Mount Elba Cemetery - inscription Shields, John B - 1815-1818
  Mount Elba Cemetery - inscription Shields, David W - 1816-1833
  Mount Elba Cemetery - inscription Shields, Dr Alfred W - 1807-1841
  Mount Elba Cemetery - inscription Shields, B P - 1820-
  Mount Elba Cemetery - inscription Shields, M J - 1821-

174   **Mount Elba Slave Block**
        same as Mount Elba

146   Muddy Creek Mill/Moon's Mill

Year	Owner
1785	Morgan, Dan
1802	James, Frederick J
1813	Bondurant, William
1847	Deane, Francis
	Rhodes, W H
	Powell, Benjamin H
	Abraham family
	Hughes family
1888	Moon family
	Moon, A F
1930	Blanton, Marion E

12   Needham

Year	Owner
before 1787	Taylor, Samuel
1787	Taylor, Creed
1832	Taylor, Mrs Creed
	Gholson, Samuel Creed
1843	Taylor, Creed & Samuel
1853	Taylor, Creed
	Taylor, Annie & Emily
1914	Howard, Mary E & A F
1916	Taylor, Emily
1916	Howard, Alfred F
1917	Harrison, Charles W
1918	Howard, Alfred F
Needham - burial	Taylor, Creed[74]

163   Newstead

Year	Owner
before 1847	Carrington, Edward
1847	Ford, Ambrose
	Ford, Beverly Buren
1930	Ford, Mrs B B

129   Northfield

Year	Owner
about 1817	Henderson, Dr Robert
	Gray, William

---

[74] Vaughan, *Crucible and Cornerstone*, 49. "Creed Taylor is buried here."

Northfield (cont.)

	1876	Gray, Andrew J
	by 1936	Gray, John Springer

129   Northfield Cemetery

	1936	Gray, Mr & Mrs
Northfield Cemetery - inscription		Perkins, Mrs Anna J - 1823-1894
Northfield Cemetery - inscription		Perkins, Judge William A - 1817-1889
Northfield Cemetery - inscription		Perkins, Baby - -1863
Northfield Cemetery - inscription		Perkins, William Allan - 1861-1862
Northfield Cemetery - inscription		Perkins, Fannie Archer - 1859-1862
Northfield Cemetery - inscription		Perkins, Robert Henderson - 1853-1854
Northfield Cemetery - inscription		Rutherford, Mary (Henderson) - 1824-1846
Northfield Cemetery - inscription		Rutherford, Robert H - 1844-1863
Northfield Cemetery - inscription		Henderson, Mrs Louisa - 1802-1870
Northfield Cemetery - inscription		Henderson, Robert, M. D. - 1795-1862
Northfield Cemetery - inscription		Page, Mrs Martha (Henderson) - 1821-1842
Northfield Cemetery - inscription		Page, Alexander T - 1819-1845

65   Oak Grove

	before 1827	Blanton, David
	1827	Blanton, James
		Wharey, Mary Blanton
	1901	Blanton, Botts
	1901	Blanton, Stuart
	1901	Blanton, Ligon
	by 1937	Blanton, Ligon & Karen

87   Oak Hill

	before 1856	Thornton, Capt William
		Thornton, Mary W
	1856	Thornton, Richard C
	1856	Thornton, John T
	1876	Booker, John A

         Subject   Year   Owner

Oak Hill (cont.)

1891	Blacker, M M & Frances
1897	Davis, Jeff
	Davis, Eugene & Alma
1906	Garvin, J B
	Amidon, W N
1915	Flippen, J B
1915	Germaine, E A
1929	Flippen, O G & Co
ca 1936	Resettlement Administration

112   Oak Hill Cemetery

Oak Hill Cemetery - inscription	Allen, Mrs Lucy - 1822-1847
Oak Hill Cemetery - inscription	Allen, Eliza - 1847-1847
Oak Hill Cemetery - inscription	Thornton, Charles Irving - 1841-1842

151   Oakland/Carrington

about 1774	Carrington, George (1738-1784)[75]
	Carrington, Codrington (ca 1760-1819)
ca 1820	Carrington, Albert[76]
after 1865	Parrish, Thomas J
1884	Parrish, Alonza J
1890	Trice, P J
1909	Funkhouser, Amos P
1922	Messinger, A E
1923	Rowh, John D
1931	Hudgins, H H
1936	Cabell, Robert Gamble III

Oakland/Carrington - inscription	Hatcher, Maria (Carrington) -[77] 1795-1857

---

[75] Brandow, *NGSQ*, 70:264. Codrington, son of George Carrington who lived at Oakland Plantation, Cumberland Co.

[76] Cumberland Co VA Order Book 1818-1821:244. 1819 Dec 27 - orphans of Codrington, Albert, Collier, and Wilson, choose Samuel Wilson as guardian.

[77] Stutesman, *Watkins Families*, 237. Maria, daughter of Codrington and Mary Ann Carrington married (1) 1818 Benjamin H Watkins. Elliott, *Marriages, Cumberland Co VA*, 65. 1832 Maria Watkins married Samuel Hatcher.

Oakland/Carrington - inscription   Carrington, Codrington -
                                        1801-1859

195 Oakland/Cocke
1731	Cocke, Bowler (1696-1771)
	Cocke, Bowler (1727-1772)[78]
1789	Cocke, William (1758-1835)
1828	Cocke, William Armistead
	Cocke, Mrs Elizabeth (Randolph)
1889	Cocke, Edmund R
1927	Cocke, E Randolph Jr

56 Oatland
before 1779	Maddox, William
1779	Harris, Joseph
1853	Goodman, Zachariah T
1879	Goodman, John W
by 1937	Goodman, Herbert

56 Oatland Antiques

see report for list of owners and
articles

188 Overton Home (Old)
before 1802	Mettauer, Joseph
1802	Gibson, Robert & Arabella
1843	Gibson, George A B
1853	Gibson, John T
1888	Wilson, Junius L
1899	Wall, J B
1904	Stuart, Walter
1909	Toff, Fred W
1919	Reid, Manus

---

[78] Dorman, *Adventurers of Purse and Person*, 1:132-3, 163-4. Bowler Cocke
(1696-1771) had a son Bowler who had a son William (1758-1835) who moved to
Cumberland Co ca 1789, resided and died at "Oakland". He married 1789 Jane
Armistead.

165   **Palmer's Tavern**
       before 1820   Johnson, Thomas & Judith
       before 1820   Johnson, Archibald & Harriet
       before 1820   Hamby, William & Judith
       1820   Johnson, Benjamin
       1851   Talley, Edwin P
       1854   Palmer, John F
       by 1936   Palmer, Mr & Mrs Bennett W

199   **Palmore Cemetery/Allen Home**
       by 1936   Allen, Mrs William
       Palmore Cemetery - inscription   Allen, Mary Elizabeth - 1843-1857
       Palmore Cemetery - inscription   Palmore, Joseph S - 1805-1846

111   **Parson's Pines** [79]
       ca 1779   ------

77   **Peabody Place (Old)**
       1843   Thackston, John
       1843   Sheppener, Mildred C
       1877   Sheppener, Clement C
       1877   Peabody, D C
       1900   Page, Martha
       1936   Page, Joseph
       1936   Whisnant, Lena

64   **Peaceful Level**
       before 1838   Walker, William
       1838   Blanton, Joseph & Susan (Walker)
                        Blanton, Mrs M B
       1909   Hughes, Mary Venable
       by 1937   Walthall, Henry C & Mary (Hughes)

48   **Pine Forest/Hughes Place**
       before 1845   Miller, William M
       before 1855   Hughes, Edward Sr
                        Hughes, Edward Jr
       by 1937   Hughes, James

---

[79] Putney, "Tar Wallet Baptist Church", 5.

173 **Pleasant Grove**

	before 1853	Anderson, Richard
	1853	Wood, John T
	1862	Broun, Dr George M
		Broun, Virginia M
	1935	Driscoll, Dr Latane
		Zimmerman, Harry M
	by 1996	Haddix, Glen & Alexus[80]

9 **Popepand/Swann Place**

	before 1752	Macon, William
	1752	Macon, Henry
	1783	Macon, Mrs Henry
	1797	Macon, William
	1797	Macon, Sallie
	1797	Swann, Sallie
		Swann, Sallie - heirs
	1886	Swann, James Singleton
	1938	Swann, J Singleton - heirs[81]

103 **Raines Tavern/Wright's Ordinary**

	before 1783	Wright, George
	1783	Wright, Henry
		Meredith, William
	1806	Raine, John
		Burke, Mrs Annie D (Raine)
	by 1936	Price, J J

98 **Refuge**

	before 1760	Taylor, Samuel
	1760	Davidson, Hezekiah
	1785	Davidson, Philemen
	1830	Minor, John
	1845	Stratton, William
	1848	Palmore, John F
	1869	Barker, Charles J
	1884	Bragg, James W

---

[80] Cox, *WPA index*, 19.

[81] Cox, *WPA index*, 23.

Refuge (cont.)

Year	Owner
1906	Talley, Ann D
1929	Talley, Abner
1935	Federal Land Bank
1935	Giles, Elizabeth

70   Reynolds Home

Year	Owner
before 1852	Talley, Zach
1852	Brown, William
	Brown, William I
1868	Reynolds, John O
1903	Byers, A M
1912	Sanderson, C R
1917	Waits, Mary
1926	Maham, Harriet
1926	Harrison, Lula
1935	Martin, John

74   Rochelle

Year	Owner
ca 1742	Lancaster Family
ca 1832	Woodson, John M
1832	Leach, J H C
	Leach, James P
1883	Taliaferro, M W
1893	Lancaster, Rev James L
1918	Putney, S W
1919	Satterwhite, S J
1919	Peace, S T
1924	Lancaster, William LeGrand
1937	Peace, Willie P
1942	Lancaster, Mrs Edwin P [82]
by 1997	Lancaster, Mrs E P & Mr & Mrs Preston

132   Rock Castle

Year	Owner
ca 1811	Nash, Thomas
1813	Nash, Thomas P

---

[82] Swinson, *Cumb. Co VA Hist Bulletin*, 12 (1997):14-5. "Rochelle was built by Lancaster ancestors and has been out of the family only briefly ...", Preston and father Edwin, and grandfather William LeGrand Lancaster.

Rock Castle (cont.)

	Year	Owner
	1834	Goodman, Robert I
	1834	Clarke, Nancy (Mrs Francis I)
		Clarke, James E
	1907	Berger, John
Rock Castle - burial		Nash, Thomas - 1782-1813

142   Rock Spring

	Year	Owner
	before 1802	Carrington, Joseph Sr
	1802	Carrington, Joseph Jr
	1811	Carrington, Paul
		Carrington, Edward
	1831	Sutphin, James
	1837	Bradley, David
	1881	Steger, Ann E (Bradley)
		Anderson, Ann (Bradley) Steger
		Carter, Mary G, J H, & M E
	1915	Abernathy, W A
	1933	Abernathy, Emma P

197   Rocky Mount

	Year	Owner
	before 1796	Lewis, Gilley
	1796	Woodson, Charles
	1804	Woodson, Jessie
	1821	Sanderson, John
	1823	Sanderson, Willie
	1843	Sanderson, Daniel
	1843	Boston, Fountain C
	1863	Hooe, Peter H
	1874	Painter, Alfred M
	1918	Burruss, R S
	1919	Ford, Mrs Annie M

140   Rosebank

	Year	Owner
	Before 1788	Woodson, Charles[83]
	ca 1830	Woodson, Tarleton

---

[83] Woodson, *Woodsons and Their Connections*, 62-4. 1788 will of Drury
Woodson gave son Charles only 5 shillings because he had previously given him
land on the Willis River on which he built Rosebank.

Rosebank (cont.)

	ca 1830	Woodson, William
	1851	Boatwright, Josiah
	1863	Johnson, William B
	1868	Johnson, Littleton T
	1871	Johnson, Ann (Mrs Littleton)
	1899	Wilkinson, Essie B & others
	1912	Case, R R
	1935	Federal Land Bank
	ca 1936	Cayce

181   Rose Cottage

	before 1852	Boatwright, Chesley
	before 1852	Carter, Jesse
	before 1852	Hudgins, John A - legatee
	before 1852	Hudgins, Elizabeth M - legatee
	before 1852	Toler, William L - legatee
	before 1852	Toler, Sarah M - legatee
	before 1852	Gilliam, Carter M - legatee
	before 1852	Palmore, Joseph - legatee
	1852	Carter, Everard
	1890	Carter, Sally (Mrs Everard)
		Toler, William B & Miller H
	by 1936	Toler, William E & Samuel

194   Rose Hill

	1783	Macon, John
		Yancy, John
	1812	Johnson, Thomas
	1816	Johnson, Watkins
	1832	Johnson, Mrs Watkins
	1832	Johnson, Richard
	1832	Johnson, Watkins
	1832	Johnson, Judith
	1832	Johnson, Eliza
	1832	Johnson, Sarah
	1832	Johnson, Martha
	1854	Adams, Armistead
	1857	Gilliam, Charles W
	1863	Crowder, William R
	1867	Crowder, John E

Rose Hill (cont.)
	1867	Diell, Caroline A
	1868	Blanton, Walker B
	1918	Blanton, Ethel
	1918	Blanton, J P

167   Scott Home/Flippen Home
	before 1855	Garrett, Samuel
	1855	Scott, Richard M
	1860	Scott, William H
	1870	Parker, Isham
	1872	Theimer, Mary - Mrs Frank
	1872	Scott, Martha Ann
	1873	Hudgins, Robert S
	1873	Southall, Walter C
	1874	Flippen, Manville A
	1912	Winifree, H Lee

167   Scott's Hill

Scott, Charles (1739-1813)[84]

20   Smith's Chapel
| | before 1814 | Smith, Robert |
| | 1814 | Trustees Methodist Episcopal Church |

67   Smith Place (Old)
	1810	Smith, Robert
	1810	Cooke, Stephen
	1842	Parrack, Segul H

---

[84] This was located in Cumberland and Powhatan Counties. An Order Book Entry, 1755: "Southam Parish wardens to bind out Charles scott orphan of Samuel Scott decd". "Notes ... Cumb Co OB 1752-1758". He married Frances Sweeney in 1762. Elliott, *Marriages, Cumberland Co VA*, 114. In 1775 a Committee of Safety resolution thanked "Captain Charles Scott and his Independent Company for their spirited Offers of their Service in defending this Colony against wicked Invaders ....". McIlwaine, *Committee of Safety Cumberland Co*, 12. Scott moved to Kentucky in 1785. It is thought that he was accompanied by Benjamin Wilson Jr whose papers date from 1785, a 1788 letter from Cumberland addressed to him at Genl Scott's in Kentucky. McCrary, *Wilson Families ... Correspondence .... 1785-1849*, 31-2.

Subject	Year	Owner

Smith Place (Old) (cont.)

	1852	Parrack, Thomas
	1852	Smith, Moses A
	1905	Smith, Peter B
	1906	Smith, J Spurgeon
	1911	Smith, Mary R
	1911	Smith, L H

177   Solitude

	before 1797	Mayo, Joseph
	before 1797	Carrington, Joseph[85]
	1797	Carrington, Benjamin
	after 1838	Carrington, Mary A E (Cabell)
	before 1840	Carrington, Joseph
	before 1841	Carrington, James L
	before 1841	Carrington, Gilbert
	before 1841	Hartsook, Elizabeth (Carrington)
	before 1842	Powell, Sophinisba (Carrington)
	before 1842	Booker, George
	before 1844	Carrington, George B
	1840-1844	Carrington, Mayo B
	1881	Carrington, Mary A E (Nelson)[86]
	1897	Hodgson, Martha P
	1909	Bonevick, Joseph
	1911	Hodgson, George P
	1911	Woodson, B B
	1911	Smith, Wm W
	1911	Winston, William Henry
	1912	Schomberg, Marion N
		Montague, J W
	1921	Schomberg, Marion N
	1923	Bedford Timber & Land Corporation

---

[85] Brandow, *NGSQ*, 70:265. Brown, *Cabells and Their Kin*, 296-7. Joseph, Benjamin and Mary Ann (Cabell).

[86] Brown, *Cabells and Their Kin*, 297. Mary A E Nelson.

Somerset Site

1755	Wilson, Benjamin (1733-1814)[87]
1815	Wilson, Willis, James, Goodrich - exrs.[88]
1815	Wilson, Dr Samuel (1770-1841)
1842	Wilson, Benjamin, Matthew & Goodrich[89]
1847	Wilson, Benjamin, Matthew & Goodrich[90]
1852-1877	Wilson, Edward[91]
before 1992	Watson[92]

189   **Southall**

before 1778	Tabb, John
before 1778	Lipscomb, Henry
1778	Southall, John
1816	Southall, Cary
1884	Parker, Isham & Ann Lou
by 1936	Parker, Early

---

[87] Cumberland Co VA Deed Book 2:260. Benjamin Wilson made his first purchase of land on the north side of Willis River. In his 1812/1814 will, he named his sons Willis, James, Samuel and Goodrich executors. In a codicil he requested that the 870 acres be sold for payment of debts to his son Samuel. Will of Benjamin Wilson, LVA.

[88] Cumberland Co VA Deed Book 13:148. The executors sell Somersett to their brother Samuel.

[89] Cumberland Co VA Will Book 10:319. In the 1841/1842 will of Samuel Wilson of Somerset, he leaves Somerset to his nephews Benjamin, Matthew and Goodridge, sons of his deceased brother Matthew. Samuel died and was buried at Somerset. Littleton Parish, Accession 29330, LVA.

[90] Cumberland Co VA Plat Book 1- 1808-1972. An 1847 plat of Summerset belonging to Ben- Mat & Goodrich Wilson containing 862 acres.

[91] Cumberland Co VA Ended Chancery Papers January term 1909. Matthew, son of Matthew, was epileptic and placed in Western Lunatic Asylum. His brother Edward, the only other one of the family to stay in Virginia was designated "Committee of Matthew Wilson". His board, fuel, lights, washing and medical attendance from 1852 until his death in 1877 were paid from the proceeds of Somerset.

[92] Visit in 1992 with Ray Watson at Bonbrook. His son lived on the site of Somerset. Somerset is mentioned frequently in the correspondence between Benjamin Wilson Jr in Kentucky and his father and brothers in Virginia. McCrary, *Wilson Families ... Correspondence .... 1785-1849.*

Subject	Year	Owner

78   Spring Hill/Cook's Tract

Year	Owner
before 1827	Wilson, Allen
1827	Wilson, John W
1875	Wilson, John W - heirs
1875	Stuart, Charlotte (Mrs D Henry)
	Stuart, David
	Stuart, Charlotte - heirs
1910	Stuart, F H
1913	Treakle, A F
1937	Richardson, E L
by 1996	Robinson, Eric L[93]

Springfield

Year	Owner
1776	Coupland, Col David O & Ann (Harrison)[94]
1794	Trent, Stephen W & Eliz. B Coupland[95]
1815	Coupland, David O Jr[96]
1850	Trent, Alexander
1880	Moseley, Mrs Trent
1888	Moseley, Trent
1890	Davis, Jeff
1907	Haggeman
1912	Crowe, Jim

70/15   Stony Point/Stony Mill Site [97]

Year	Owner
before 1808	Skipwith, William
1808	Harrison, Edmund
1816	Trent, John
1816	Woodson, James B
1824	Langhorne, Maurice Jr
1824	Palmore, John R
1827	Palmore, Charles S

---

[93] Cox, *WPA index*, 22.

[94] Stanard, *Genealogies, Virginia Magazine*, 3:744, 831. "Their home was Springfield lying in both Cumberland and Buckingham Counties".

[95] Brown, *Genealogy .... Wilson*, 5. Stephen W Trent married Eliz. B Coupland in 1794 at Springfield.

[96] The rest of the names and dates come from the Buckingham report on Springfield, BU355.

[97] *Cumb Co VA and Its People*, 34.

Stony Point/Stony Mill Site (cont.)

	1827	Fuqua, Joseph
	1887	Palmore, E R
	1889	Wood, Dr Richard
	before 1907	Wood, Cabell S
	before 1907	Wood, Warrington
	1907	Davis, Thaddeus Lee
	after 1907	Davis, Martha Maria & children

123   Talley Home

	before 1763	Robinson, John
	1763	Robinson, Edward
	1805	Miller, John
	1808	Anderson, Lewis
	1811	Dunkum, John
	1815	Talley, Jack
	before 1908	Talley, Nelson - heirs
	1908	Robinson, Jeffrey

128   Tar Wallet Church [98]

	by 1732	Church of England
	after 1776	All Denominations
	1904	Methodists
	1943	Baptists
	1935	Harlan, Mrs Max B Sr[99]

1   Thackston Home (Old) [100]

	before 1857	Marshall, H H
	1857	Warren, Howell E
	1860	Thackston, Elizabeth Rosa
		Thackston, Richard D
	1924	Davidson, N B
	1937	Davidson - heirs
	by 1998	Putney, Fred W
	by 1998	Putney, Walter G

---

[98] Putney, "Tar Wallet Baptist Church".

[99] Putney, "Tar Wallet Baptist Church", 7.

[100] *Cumb. Co VA Hist Bulletin*, 13 (1998):15.

145   Thomas Chapel [101]

before 1840	Maddox, William G
1846	Hatcher, Samuel - trustee
1846	Woodson, Tarleton - trustee
1846	Talley, Dr Zack - trustee
1846	Maddox, Thomas - trustee
1846	Brown, William I - trustee
1846	Sanderson, Obadiah - trustee
1846	Walton, Nathaniel - trustee

113   Trenton/Brick House

about 1825	Trent, Dr John (1789-1862)[102]
1886	Auditor of Public Accounts
1900	Gray, B H
1903	Trent, J A & A L
1903	Moses, Julia L
1903	Trent, W J
1908	Bowe, Bruce & Caroline
1908	Flood, H D
1909	Lancaster, William & Mary E
1913	Freese, Henry T
1933	Farrier, L W
1936	Resettlement Administration
Trenton - inscription	Trent, Mary B - 1815-1856

138   Trenton Mill/Sport's Lake

before 1750	Basset, Thomas[103]
1750	Gray, William
1752	Basset, Nathaniel
1790	Trent, Alexander
	Trent, Peterfield
1794	Trent, John A
1823	Brown, Daniel
1836	McAshan, John T

---

[101] *Cumb. Co VA Hist Bulletin*, 12 (1997):16.

[102] *Notes on Peter Field Trent.*

[103] Known as Randolph Creek Mill.

Trenton Mill/Sport's Lake (cont.)

Year	Owner
1841	Robinson, John & Ann[104]
1841	Trent, John L
1842	Jackson, Peter
1848	Johnson, David & Susan
1855	Wilkinson, Ducalion
1860	Wilkinson, Jane
	Putney, Rosa I & her husband
1880	Wilkinson, George T
1880	Bondurant, Mollie P
1903	Wilkinson, George T
1906	Brown, A T
1911	Brown, Mary L
1913	Phillips, Malcolm & Cecil
1933	Johnson, A Martin

118 Trent's Mill

Year	Owner
after 1767	Trent, Alexander (1758-1804)[105]
ca 1804	Trent, Mary Anne
after 1808	Page, John C & Mary Anne (Trent)
1838	Trent, William A
1843	Trent, Stephen W
1843	Trent, William A
1843	Wilson, John P
1845	Wilson, William W
	Wilson, Edward[106]
1867	Page, Reynolds & A C
1885	Bateman, Margaret L & Elkanar
	Bateman, Adriana
1901	Keller, D A

---

[104] Known as Burr Mills on Randolph Creek.

[105] Avant, *Southern Colonial Families*, 4:749-750. Trent Bible.

[106] This may have to do with Edward Wilson, "Committee of Matthew Wilson". Cumberland Co VA Ended Chancery Papers January term 1909. See Somerset. Edward was also a descendant of Alexander Trent.

193   **Underhill Site**
               before 1807   Allen, Daniel (1728-1807) - probably[107]
               ca 1807   Wilson, Richard (1752-1827)[108]
               ca 1827   Wilson, Allen (1780-1849)
               1847   Armistead, Dr Thomas D
               abt 1865   Armistead, Martha (Wilson)
               1886   Miller, J F & wife
               1886   Armistead, James A
               1894   Lowman, Fannie A
               1894   Armistead, James A
               1914   Armistead, James A Jr

115   **Union Hill**
               1748   Anderson, Samuel Sr
                                Anderson, Samuel Jr
                                Page, John C[109]
               about 1853   Page, Mary A (Trent)
               after 1877   Daniel, Mary Ann (Page)
               after 1877   Kinckle, Maria W (Page)
               after 1877   Page, Harriet R
                                Randolph, D Coupland & Harriet (Page)
               before 1915   Randolph, D Coupland Jr
               before 1915   Randolph, Beverly
               before 1915   Randolph, Mary A
               1915   Piedmont Lumber Co
               1918   Trent, Stephen W
               ca 1936   Federal Land Bank

115   **Union Hill Cemetery**
                                Page family
       Union Hill Cemetery - inscription   Page, Eliza Trent - 1815-1838
       Union Hill Cemetery - inscription   Page, Ellen Cary - 1817-1837
       Union Hill Cemetery - inscription   Page, Archibald Cary - 1824-1871

---

[107] Watkins, *Tearin' Through the Wilderness*, 127. Daniel Allen.

[108] Cumberland Co VA Will Book 8:264. 1826/1827 will of Richard Wilson named his sons Allen Wilson and Daniel Allen Wilson.

[109] Brown, *Genealogy ... Wilson*, 2-3. Anna Trent married John C Page and raised ... Mary Ann (Mrs John Daniel), ... Maria (Mrs Kinckle), ... Harriet (Mrs D C Randolph)". Carlton, "History of Trent Family", 6 (Cumb Co Deed Book 39:70-1).

Union Hill Cemetery - inscription   Page, Lucy A (Trent) - 1826-1853
Union Hill Cemetery - inscription   Page, John C - 1784-1853

141   **Viewmont**
                1936   Haines, Travis

58   **Walnut Hill**
                before 1755   Durham, John
                1755   Dupuy, John James
                                  Dupuy, John
                1878   Jones, Rebecca E
                1882   Lancaster, William L
                                  Lancaster, Susan G (Mrs Wm L)
                                  Lancaster, J P (son)
                1909   Crute, H C

158   **Walton's Mill**
                1765   Carrington, George
                1785   Carrington, Nathaniel
                1803   Carrington, Phoebe (Harris)
                ca 1808   Walton, Frances Ann (Carrington)[110]
                ca 1808   Pittman, Henningham (Carrington)
                1830   Walton, Thomas H
                1845   Noel, John & Mary
                1848   Robinson, Alfred D
                1856   Wood, John T
                1858   Flanagan, Madison F
                                  Flanagan, William H
                1893   Trice, Phillip I
                by 1936   Trice, Benjamin

14   **West Hill**
                1798   Eppes, Francis
                ca 1808   Eggleston, Edmond[111]
                                  Eggleston, Stephen
                ca 1854   Scott, Joseph

---

[110] Dorman, *Adventurers of Purse and Person*,1:421. "Phoebe died about 1808".
[111] *Today and Yesterday*, 286. Gives details of Egglestons, Joseph Scott, and graveyard.

West Hill (cont.)

	1855	Blanton, Dr Philip S
	by 1937	Blanton, Dr Charles A
West Hill - graveyard		Eggleston, Edmond & wife
West Hill - graveyard		Eggleston
West Hill - graveyard		Armistead, Rev Jesse S - infant children

37/53   White Hall/Walker Place/Cemetery

before 1752	Walker, William
1752	Walker, Warren
1785	Walker, William
1828	Walker, William B B
1870	Walker, William D
1879	Walker, William D - widow
	Walker, Ellen M - heirs
1929	Walker, H S & W D

161   White Level

before 1811	Hughes, John
1811	Mitchell, Cary
1845	Smith, Henry
1848	Smith, William E
1849	Miller, James & Virginia
1852	Brown, Samuel
1897	Snead, Dr N P

139   Wilkinson Cemetery

	Wilkinson family
Wilkinson Cemetery - inscription	Wilkinson, B S - -1860
Wilkinson Cemetery - inscription	Wilkinson, D - -1860
Wilkinson Cemetery - inscription	Wilkinson, R H - -1872

28   Willow Bank/McGehee

before 1848	McGehee, Thomas B
1848	Hazlegrove, Winston
	Hazlegrove, Charles et al
1872	Blanton, Joseph
	Hughes, Thomas W
1883	Blanton, Camilla F
1911	Blanton, Dr Hugh L

Willow Bank/McGehee (cont.)

	1912	Blanton, H L Jr
	by 1937	Blanton, Mrs H L

75 Willow Bank/Isbell

	1811	Isbell, Lewis
	1830	Isbell, James
	1848	Isbell, James D
	1849	Mosby, William G & Amelia[112]
	1849	Isbell, Thomas M & Frances A
	1870	Woodson, B B
	1873	Fowlkes, Joseph M
	1873	Flippen, John T
	1890	Flippen, Mary Ann & daughters
	1904	Goodman, William I & Pocahontas V
	1919	Smith, William M
	1919	McRae, Donald
	1919	Jarrett, D L
	1926	Jarrett, Thomas W
	1926	Stover, Mr & Mrs Wm C
	1926	Jarrett, Mr & Mrs Wm P
	1926	Roberts, Mr & Mrs
	1926	Phillips, Mrs Fannie Myrtle
	1937	Mering, Mrs Myrtle Phillips

71 Womack Place (Old)

	before 1811	Womack, Charles
	1839	Lee, William
	1850	Sims, Edward B
	1851	Smith, John M
	by 1937	Smith, Arthur J

166 Woodbourne/Beech Run

	before 1843	Goodman, Wilson N
	1843	Goodman, Thomas B
	1844	Sanderson, Thomas B
	1854	Harrison, Dr Edward J
	1903	Harrison, Dr Edward J - heirs

---

[112] Cox, *WPA index*, 26. Wives names added.

Woodbourne/Beech Run (cont.)

	by 1936	Rodgers, Mrs Kate

25/38   Woodlawn/Cooper

	before 1846	Cooper, Thomas
	1846	Ford, Hezekiah
	1851	Diggs, Thomas
	1858	Ford, Hezekiah
	1868	Brown, Eleanor Ford
	1888	Flippen, John
	1910	Stout, Charles A
	1910	Stout, Walter C

Woodlawn/Cooper Cemetery - burial   Ford, Hezekiah - after 1850

33   Woodlawn/Epps

	before 1800	Epps, Francis
	1800	Walker, Elizabeth (Epps)
		Walker, David & Elizabeth
	1804	Keeble, Walter & Sally
	1808	Daniel, William
	1812	Isbell, Lewis
	1827	Isbell, Lewis M & Eliza A
	1848	McGehee, Thomas B & Lucy Ann
	1851	Scott, Joel J
	1857	Wilson, Thomas Friend
	1862	Miller, Giles A & Martha S
	1863	Crowder, Harriet
	1882	Crowder, Thomas W
		Crowder, Rebecca (Jeter)
	1925	Womack, Nathan

182   Woodlawn/Ross

	before 1810	Ross, David
	1810	Duffield, John
	1834	Ross, Frederick
	1835	Lewis, Benjamin
	1841	Goodman, Joseph N
	1859	Watkins, Richard V & Polly
	1863	Smith, Augustine I
	1869	Shelton, John M
	1873	Loveing, Seaton H

Woodlawn/Ross (cont.)

	1873	Shelton, John M
	by 1876	Baker, John M
	1898	Baker, Irvine
	1912	Mills, W R
	1914	Chisolm, Edna E & W A

27 Woodside Site

	before 1800	Booker, Edward
	1800	Booker, Edith C
	1838	Booker, William
		Booker, John A
	1883	Trent, Isaiah
	1887	Reynolds, John O
	1899	Smith, George E B
	1903	Flippen, Robert Alice

92 Woodville Site

	before 1843	Wilson, Allen & wife
	before 1843	Wilson, John W & wife
	1843	Flourney, John James
		Flourney, P H & W C
	1847	Armistead, Martha S (Mrs Jesse S)
	1870	Hawkins, J L
	1870	Hawkins, Hannah B
	1870	Hawkins, Amelia M
	1876	Whitehead, I P & wife
	1876	Whitehead, F A
	1880	Dabney, Charles V & wife
	1891	Dabney, Charles
	1899	Womack, Charles

Index by Owner

Owner	Year	Subject
Anderson, Charles	before 1759	Cumberland Presbyterian Church
Anderson, daughter m E J Harrison		Morningside
Anderson, Elijah G	ca 1881	Clifton/Harrison
Anderson, Elijah G	1878	Morningside
Anderson, Jesse	before 1813	Foster Graveyard (Old)
Anderson, Jesse	1813	Midway/Langhorne's Home
Anderson, Jessie	before 1814	Mountain View/Meador Place
Anderson, Lewis	1808	Talley Home
Anderson, Richard	before 1853	Pleasant Grove
Anderson, Richard I	1839	Hudgins Tavern/Locust Grove
Anderson, Sallie		Hudgins Tavern/Locust Grove
Anderson, Samuel Jr		Union Hill
Anderson, Samuel Sr	1748	Union Hill
Anderson, Theodore C	before 1912	Clifton/Harrison
Anderson, Wister	1912	Clifton/Harrison
Anderson, Wister & Hildreth	1887	Hudgins Tavern/Locust Grove
Arden, John	1908	Melrose
Armistead, Dr Thomas D	1847	Underhill Site
Armistead, James A	1886	Underhill Site
Armistead, James A	1894	Underhill Site
Armistead, James A Jr	1914	Underhill Site
Armistead, Martha (Wilson)	abt 1865	Underhill Site
Armistead, Martha S (Mrs Jesse S)	1847	Woodville Site
Armistead, Rev Jesse S - infant children		West Hill - graveyard
Armstead, Anderson	1842	Ca Ira Mill
Armstead, James A	1836	Ca Ira Mill
Armstrong, A B - comr.	1904	Blanton Home (Old)
Atkins, W T	1935	Jiltic Farm/Booker's Mill
Atkinson, Betty Carr (Harrison) - 1826-1847		Clifton Cemetery - inscription
Atkinson, Peyton Harrison - 1812-1848		Clifton Cemetery - inscription
Auditor of Public Accounts	1886	Trenton/Brick House
Austin, James	before 1792	Austin Home
Austin, James M	1843	Dawson Home

Owner	Year	Subject
Austin, John A		
& Frances (Meador)	1839	Austin Home
Austin, William	1792	Austin Home
Austin, William		
& Judith (Atkinson)	1794	Austin Home
Badgett, Nannie T	1904	Millview
Bagby, Mrs Lillian	1882	Austin Home
Baker, German	1806	Mill Mount
Baker, I M	1924	Ampthill
Baker, I M	1927	Ampthill
Baker, Irvine	1898	Woodlawn/Ross
Baker, Jerman	1815	Cherry Grove/Thweatt
Baker, John M	by 1876	Woodlawn/Ross
Ballew, Charles	1814	Felixville
Baltimore, Christopher	before 1810	Cedar Plains
Bank of South Boston	by 1937	Millview
Barker, Charles J	1869	Refuge
Barker, Charles J - heirs		Irwin's Tavern Site
Barker, Joseph M et al	1896	Irwin's Tavern Site
Barker, W J	1902	Irwin's Tavern Site
Basset, Nathaniel	1752	Trenton Mill/Sport's Lake
Basset, Thomas	before 1750	Trenton Mill/Sport's Lake
Bateman, Adriana		Trent's Mill
Bateman, Margaret L		
& Elkanar	1885	Trent's Mill
Bates, John B	1919	Cherry Grove/Thweatt
Beale, John J	1864	Gravel Hill
Beatty, Francis I	1874	Fork, The
Bedford Timber & Land		
Corporation	1923	Solitude
Belmore, Chris	1913	Englewood/Horn Quarter
Berger, John	1907	Rock Castle
Berkeley, Ellen	1870	High Hill
Berkeley, Ellen (Wilson)	1870	Hors du Monde
Berry, Oscar H	1911	Glentivar
Blacker, M M & Frances	1891	Oak Hill
Blake, James C	1859	Corson Home/Coupland's Tavern
Blanton, Botts	1901	Oak Grove
Blanton, Camilla F	1883	Willow Bank/McGehee
Blanton, David	before 1827	Oak Grove

Owner	Year	Subject
Blanton, Dr Charles A	by 1937	West Hill
Blanton, Dr Hugh L	1911	Willow Bank/McGehee
Blanton, Dr Philip S	1855	West Hill
Blanton, Eliza D	1886	Cherry Grove/Thweatt
Blanton, Eliza D - heirs		Cherry Grove/Thweatt
Blanton, Ethel	1918	Rose Hill
Blanton, H L Jr	1912	Willow Bank/McGehee
Blanton, J J		Guinea Mills
Blanton, J P	1918	Rose Hill
Blanton, James	1827	Oak Grove
Blanton, James M	1845	Millview
Blanton, James W	1870	High Hill
Blanton, Jas W	1870	High Hill
Blanton, Joe	by 1937	Guinea Mills
Blanton, John	1821	Midway/Langhorne's Home
Blanton, John James - 1848-1909		Guinea Mills - inscription
Blanton, John R - 1881-1930		Guinea Mills - inscription
Blanton, Joseph	1867	Briarfield
Blanton, Joseph	1867	Guinea Mills
Blanton, Joseph	1872	Willow Bank/McGehee
Blanton, Joseph & Susan (Walker)	1838	Peaceful Level
Blanton, Laura P - 1854-1924		Guinea Mills - inscription
Blanton, Ligon	1901	Oak Grove
Blanton, Ligon & Karen	by 1937	Oak Grove
Blanton, Marion E	1930	Muddy Creek Mill/Moon's Mill
Blanton, Mrs H L	by 1937	Willow Bank/McGehee
Blanton, Mrs M B		Peaceful Level
Blanton, S J		Millview
Blanton, Stuart	1901	Oak Grove
Blanton, Thomas W	1873	Blanton Home (Old)
Blanton, Walker B	1868	Rose Hill
Blunt, Annie E	1908	Glentivar
Boatwright, Chesley	before 1852	Rose Cottage
Boatwright, Josiah	1851	Rosebank
Bogert, George W	1870	Morven
Bogert, Miss Lilly	after 1871	Morven
Bondurant, Mollie P	1880	Trenton Mill/Sport's Lake
Bondurant, William	1813	Muddy Creek Mill/Moon's Mill

Owner	Year	Subject
Bonevick, Joseph	1909	Solitude
Booker, Anderson	1819	Booker's Mill
Booker, Bernard	1811	Booker's Mill
Booker, E Nash - -1868		Booker Cemetery (Old) - inscription
Booker, Edith C	1800	Woodside Site
Booker, Edward		Booker Cemetery (Old)
Booker, Edward	1785	Booker's Mill
Booker, Edward	1819	Booker's Mill
Booker, Edward	before 1842	Bookers Tavern
Booker, Edward	before 1800	Woodside Site
Booker, Fannie Munford - 1884-1904		Booker Cemetery (Old) - inscription
Booker, Frederick		Bookers Tavern
Booker, George	1838	Cedar Plains
Booker, George	before 1842	Solitude
Booker, John A	1876	Oak Hill
Booker, John A		Woodside Site
Booker, Mrs Thomas	1850	Bookers Tavern
Booker, Pink - trustee	1811	Felixville
Booker, Rev George E - 1828-1899		Booker Cemetery (Old) - inscription
Booker, Richard	1829	Booker's Mill
Booker, Richard - trustee	1811	Felixville
Booker, Samuel	1838	Cedar Plains
Booker, Thomas	1842	Bookers Tavern
Booker, William		Booker Cemetery (Old)
Booker, William	1838	Woodside Site
Booker, William N		Bookers Tavern
Bosher, John C	1820	Corson Home/Coupland's Tavern
Boston, Fountain C	1843	Rocky Mount
Bowe, Bruce & Caroline	1908	Trenton/Brick House
Bowe, R Patrick & Virginia	by 1991	Clay Bank
Bowles, James Cocke	1904	Hooper's Rock
Bowles, James Cocke Jr	by 1936	Hooper's Rock
Bradley, David	1837	Rock Spring
Bragg, James W	1884	Refuge
Bransford, Benjamin - trustee	1811	Felixville
Bransford, Francis		Frayser's Tavern
Bransford, Jacob - trustee	1811	Felixville

Owner	Year	Subject
Branton, William A	1854	Englewood/Horn Quarter
Brazeal Family		Frayser's Tavern
Brereton, Mrs Ethel (Watkins)	1911	Langhorne's Tavern
Brock, Lucy A		Hooper's Rock
Broun, Dr George M	1862	Pleasant Grove
Broun, Virginia M		Pleasant Grove
Brown, A L Jr	1914	Hors du Monde
Brown, A L Jr - widow & daughter	1918	Hors du Monde
Brown, A T	1912	Chow Chow /Phillips Home
Brown, A T	1906	Trenton Mill/Sport's Lake
Brown, Abram T	1895	Glentivar
Brown, Daniel	1823	Trenton Mill/Sport's Church
Brown, Davis	before 1774	Brown's Presbyterian Church
Brown, Eleanor Ford	1868	Woodlawn/Cooper
Brown, John	1814	Felixville
Brown, Mary L	1911	Trenton Mill/Sport's Lake
Brown, Samuel	1852	White Level
Brown, William	1852	Reynolds Home
Brown, William I		Reynolds Home
Brown, William I - trustee	1846	Thomas Chapel
Bryan, Maggie	1932	Auburn
Bryant, A J, W C, Edward, Silas, Willie		Cedar Grove/Bryant Place
Bryant, Isaac	before 1799	Cedar Grove/Bryant Place
Bryant, James	1799	Cedar Grove/Bryant Place
Bryant, Silas		Cedar Grove/Bryant Place
Bryant, Silas S	1858	Gravel Hill
Budd, H H	1878	Burleigh Hall
Burke, Mrs Annie D (Raine)		Raines Tavern/Wright's Ordinary
Burruss, R S	1918	Rocky Mount
Byers, A M	1903	Reynolds Home
Cabell, Robert Gamble III	1936	Oakland/Carrington
Caldwell, John	1823	Glebe, The
Calland, Joseph	1767	Langhorne's Tavern
Carnes, Everett A	1933	Broomfield/Steger's Farm
Carnes, W Sherman	1933	Broomfield/Steger's Farm
Carnes, W W	1911	Broomfield/Steger's Farm

Owner	Year	Subject
Carrington, Albert	ca 1820	Oakland/Carrington
Carrington, Ann (Adams)	1803	Boston Hill
Carrington, Benjamin	1809	Boston Hill
Carrington, Benjamin	1827	Cedar Plains
Carrington, Benjamin	1797	Solitude
Carrington, Codrington	before 1859	Melrose
Carrington, Codrington - 1801-1859		Oakland/Carrington - inscription
Carrington, Codrington (ca 1760-1819)		Oakland/Carrington
Carrington, Edward	1806	Ca Ira Mill
Carrington, Edward	before 1847	Newstead
Carrington, Edward		Rock Spring
Carrington, George	1765	Walton's Mill
Carrington, George - vestryman	1772	Glebe, The - Church of England
Carrington, George (1711-1785)	after 1732	Boston Hill
Carrington, George (1738-1784)	about 1774	Oakland/Carrington
Carrington, George B	before 1844	Solitude
Carrington, George Jr - vestryman	1772	Glebe, The - Church of England
Carrington, Gilbert	before 1841	Solitude
Carrington, James L	before 1841	Solitude
Carrington, James L (1813-.....)		Elkora/Walnut Hill
Carrington, James S & Ann M	1838	Cedar Plains
Carrington, Joseph - Tavern-Keeper	1774	Effingham House
Carrington, Joseph	before 1797	Solitude
Carrington, Joseph	before 1840	Solitude
Carrington, Joseph - vestryman	1772	Glebe, The - Church of England
Carrington, Joseph Jr	1802	Rock Spring
Carrington, Joseph Sr	before 1802	Rock Spring
Carrington, Mary A E (Cabell)	after 1838	Solitude
Carrington, Mary A E (Nelson)	1881	Solitude
Carrington, Mayo (1753-1803)	1785	Boston Hill
Carrington, Mayo B - trustee	1856	Fork of Willis Church
Carrington, Mayo B	1840-1844	Solitude

Owner	Year	Subject
Carrington, Mayo B & Mary Ann	1838	Cedar Plains
Carrington, Nathaniel	1785	Walton's Mill
Carrington, Paul	1811	Rock Spring
Carrington, Phoebe (Harris)	1803	Walton's Mill
Carrington, William	1838	Cedar Plains
Carruthers, Lizzie B	before 1926	Glen Mary
Carter, Everard	1852	Rose Cottage
Carter, Jesse	before 1852	Rose Cottage
Carter, Mary G, J H, & M E		Rock Spring
Carter, Robert	1723	Glentivar
Carter, Sally (Mrs Everard)	1890	Rose Cottage
Cary, Henry	before 1735	Barter Hill
Case, R R	1912	Rosebank
Cayce	ca 1936	Rosebank
Cayce, Fleming	before 1807	Corson Home/Coupland's Tavern
Chappell, Albert	1885	Midway/Langhorne's Home
Chappell, Varina E (Mrs Albert)	before 1937	Midway/Langhorne's Home
Cheshire, Benjamin	1797	Langhorne's Tavern
Cheshire, Benjamin B	1797	Foster Place (Old)/Hobson Place
Cheshire, Benjamin B	before 1812	Midway/Langhorne's Home
Chisolm, Edna E & W A	1914	Woodlawn/Ross
Clairborne, Lula H	1912	Blanton Home (Old)
Clarke, Francis I	1814	Felixville
Clarke, James E	1894	Goshen
Clarke, James E		Rock Castle
Clarke, James E - heirs		Goshen
Clarke, Nancy (Mrs Francis I)	1834	Rock Castle
Clarke, Thomas B	1846	Goshen
Clarke, Thomas B - heirs		Goshen
Cocke, Bowler (1696-1771)	1731	Oakland/Cocke
Cocke, Bowler (1727-1772)		Oakland/Cocke
Cocke, E Randolph Jr	1927	Oakland/Cocke
Cocke, Edmund R	1889	Oakland/Cocke
Cocke, Mrs Elizabeth (Randolph)		Oakland/Cocke
Cocke, William (1758-1835)	1789	Oakland/Cocke
Cocke, William Armistead	1828	Oakland/Cocke

Owner	Year	Subject
Coleman, Gulielmus	before 1797	Foster Place (Old)/Hobson Place
Coleman, Gulielmus	1794	Langhorne's Tavern
Colley, Mrs Lenora	1843	Cedar Bluff/Scott Place
Colley, William Jr	1828	Cedar Bluff/Scott Place
Colley, William W	1832	Cedar Bluff/Scott Place
Colquitt, John - trustee	1811	Felixville
Colwell, James Madison - 1793		Colwell Graveyard - inscription
Cook, Stephen	1828	Booker's Mill
Cooke, Stephen	1810	Smith Place (Old)
Cooper, Thomas	before 1846	Woodlawn/Cooper
Corson, Charles	by 1936	Corson Home/Coupland's Tavern
Corson, Mary A	1848	Glebe, The
Corson, William C & Jennie H		Glebe, The
Coupland, Col David O & Ann (Harrison)	1776	Springfield
Coupland, David O Jr	1815	Springfield
Coupland, William R	1822	Corson Home/Coupland's Tavern
Cowherd, Thomas E	1901	Broomfield/Steger's Farm
Crawley, Charles W - 18?5-1890		Guinea Church Cemetery - inscription
Crawley, Hanna Fennell - 1867-1929		Guinea Church Cemetery - inscription
Crawley, Maggie Tinsley - 1844-1911		Guinea Church Cemetery - inscription
Crawley, Thomas Lilburn - 1916-1917		Guinea Church Cemetery - inscription
Crowder, Harriet	1863	Meador's Store/Old Store
Crowder, Harriet	1863	Woodlawn/Epps
Crowder, John E	1851	Locust Grove Cemetery
Crowder, John E	1851	Locust Grove/Nelson
Crowder, John E	1867	Rose Hill
Crowder, Rebecca (Jeter)		Woodlawn/Epps
Crowder, T W		Jiltic Farm/Booker's Mill
Crowder, Thomas W	1845	Buena Vista Site
Crowder, Thomas W	1822	Locust Grove/Nelson
Crowder, Thomas W	1825	Locust Grove/Nelson
Crowder, Thomas W	1845	Meador's Store/Old Store

Owner	Year	Subject
Crowder, Thomas W	before 1839	Mountain View/Locust Level
Crowder, Thomas W	1882	Woodlawn/Epps
Crowder, Thomas Wilson	1825	Locust Grove Cemetery
Crowder, Thomas Wilson - 1795-1855		Locust Grove Cemetery - inscription
Crowder, William B	1833	Forkland
Crowder, William B	1835	Forkland
Crowder, William R	1863	Buena Vista Site
Crowder, William R	1863	Meador's Store/Old Store
Crowder, William R	1863	Rose Hill
Crowe, Jim	1912	Springfield
Crute, H C	1909	Walnut Hill
Crute, J M	1904	Blanton Home (Old)
Crute, J V	1873	High Hill
Cullen, William T	1891	Englewood/Horn Quarter
Cunningham, Edward	1827	Burleigh Hall
Cunningham, Jane	before 1827	Burleigh Hall
Cunningham, John A	1833	Morven
Cunningham, Richard	before 1810	Burleigh Hall
Cushing, Catherine Thornton - 1833-1834		Fork Cemetery - inscription
Dabney, Charles	1891	Woodville Site
Dabney, Charles V & wife	1880	Woodville Site
Dame, George Washington - 1858-1859		Fork Cemetery - inscription
Daniel, Dr W S	1895	Jiltic Farm/Booker's Mill
Daniel, Mary Ann (Page)	after 1877	Union Hill
Daniel, Robert & Louisa	before 1856	Fork of Willis Church
Daniel, William	1808	Woodlawn/Epps
Davidson - heirs	1937	Thackston Home (Old)
Davidson, Hezekiah	1760	Refuge
Davidson, N B	1924	Thackston Home (Old)
Davidson, Philemen	1785	Refuge
Davis, E R	1903	Englewood/Horn Quarter
Davis, E R	1906	Englewood/Horn Quarter
Davis, E R	before 1919	Englewood/Horn Quarter
Davis, Eugene & Alma		Oak Hill
Davis, Jeff	1897	Oak Hill
Davis, Jeff	1890	Springfield
Davis, Kate	1924	Cedar Plains
Davis, Martha Maria & children	after 1907	Stony Point/Stony Mill Site

Owner	Year	Subject
Davis, R T	1903	Bonbrook
Davis, Rebecca - Bryant/Oliver, heirs		Cedar Grove/Bryant Place
Davis, Robert	1903	Bonbrook Cemetery
Davis, Thaddeus Lee	1907	Stony Point/Stony Mill Site
Dawson, Catherine M	1845	Dawson Home
Dawson, Lewis		Dawson Home
Dawson, Mrs Ella R	1892	Dawson Home
Day, George K		Melrose
Deane, Anne H - 1768-1833		Deanery Cemetery - inscription
Deane, Francis	1795	Ca Ira Mill
Deane, Francis	1847	Muddy Creek Mill/Moon's Mill
Deane, Francis B - 1770-1860		Deanery Cemetery - inscription
Deane, Francis Browne	ca 1791	Deanery, The
Deane, Francis Browne - heirs	after 1860	Deanery, The
Deane, Francis Browne Jr - 1796-1868		Deanery Cemetery - inscription
Deane, James	1795	Ca Ira Mill
Deane, Thomas	1795	Ca Ira Mill
Dickey, George S	1909	Broomfield/Steger's Farm
Diell, Caroline A	1867	Rose Hill
Diggs, Charles D	1892	Dunleith
Diggs, Mrs Sterling	1937	Hickory Hall
Diggs, Thomas	1851	Woodlawn/Cooper
Dillon, Mildred	1993	Barter Hill
Dowdy, R J	1906	Ca Ira Mill
Driscoll, Dr Latane	1935	Pleasant Grove
Duffield, John	1810	Woodlawn/Ross
Duncan, P L	1931	Hudgins Tavern/Locust Grove
Duncan, W S	1883	Boston Hill
Dunkum, John	1811	Talley Home
Dupuy, John		Walnut Hill
Dupuy, John James	1755	Walnut Hill
Durham, John	before 1755	Walnut Hill
Easeley, Wharam & Elizabeth	1747	Glebe, The
Easeley, William	before 1747	Glebe, The
Easterly, D E	1934	Chow Chow /Phillips Home
Edwards, Daniel C	before 1830	Ashland

Owner	Year	Subject
Eggleston		West Hill - graveyard
Eggleston, Edmond	ca 1808	West Hill
Eggleston, Edmond & wife		West Hill - graveyard
Eggleston, Edmund	1806	Mill Mount
Eggleston, Edmund - founder	1825	Guinea Church/Tuggle's Meeting House
Eggleston, Richard S - Tavern-Keeper	1817	Effingham House
Eggleston, Stephen		West Hill
Ehrhart, Mary (Carnes)	1921	Broomfield/Steger's Farm
Ehrlich, Emil	1903	Burleigh Hall
Elam, Irving G	1926	Glen Mary
Elam, James B	1901	Glen Mary
Elam, Mary E	1878	Glen Mary
Eliza and Dilcy, faithful servants		Farmview - inscription
Emerson Family	after 1922	Englewood/Horn Quarter
England, William	1819	Booker's Mill
Eppes, Francis	1798	West Hill
Eppes, John W	1810	Cherry Grove/Thweatt
Epps, Francis	before 1800	Woodlawn/Epps
Farrier, L W	1933	Trenton/Brick House
Farris, Jacob - trustee	1811	Felixville
Federal Land Bank	1922	Englewood/Horn Quarter
Federal Land Bank	before 1934	Englewood/Horn Quarter
Federal Land Bank		Felixville
Federal Land Bank	1929	Goshen
Federal Land Bank		Hudgins Tavern/Locust Grove
Federal Land Bank	1936	Langhorne's Tavern
Federal Land Bank	1925	Mill Mount
Federal Land Bank	1932	Mountain View/Locust Level
Federal Land Bank	1935	Refuge
Federal Land Bank	1935	Rosebank
Federal Land Bank	ca 1936	Union Hill
Fendley, David "at the courthouse" - Tavern-Keeper	1780	Effingham House
Ferris		Jesse Thomas Site
Fitzgerald, Nace		Cedar Bluff/Scott Place
Fitzpatrick, Thomas & Mary Ann	1838	Cedar Plains

Owner	Year	Subject
Flanagan, James Montague	1900	Cedar Plains
Flanagan, Madison	1924	Cedar Plains
Flanagan, Madison - trustee	1856	Fork of Willis Church
Flanagan, Madison	1865	Gravel Hill
Flanagan, Madison F	1853	Cedar Plains
Flanagan, Madison F	1858	Walton's Mill
Flanagan, Plummer	1924	Cedar Plains
Flanagan, R S	1936	McCullough Tombstone
Flanagan, Robert	1924	Cedar Plains
Flanagan, William H		Walton's Mill
Fleming, Elizabeth	1874	Mount Airy
Flippen, Amanda F	1867	Locust Grove/Flippen
Flippen, Arthur	by 1936	Flippen Home
Flippen, Herman	by 1936	Flippen Home
Flippen, J B	1915	Oak Hill
Flippen, James	1831	Briarfield
Flippen, James	before 1831	Guinea Mills
Flippen, James - heirs	before 1831	Guinea Mills
Flippen, James W	1832	Flippen Home
Flippen, James W Jr		Flippen Home
Flippen, John	1888	Woodlawn/Cooper
Flippen, John T	1873	Willow Bank/Isbell
Flippen, Manville A	1874	Scott Home/Flippen Home
Flippen, Mary Ann & daughters	1890	Willow Bank/Isbell
Flippen, Menville A		Flippen Home
Flippen, Mrs Alice (Morrison)	1895	Burleigh Hall
Flippen, O G	1907	Chow Chow /Phillips Home
Flippen, O G & Co	1929	Oak Hill
Flippen, Robert Alice	1903	Woodside Site
Flippen, W C	1924	Mount Airy
Flippen, William	1811	Locust Grove/Flippen
Flood, H D	1908	Trenton/Brick House
Flourney, John James	1843	Woodville Site
Flourney, P H & W C		Woodville Site
Ford, Ambrose	1847	Newstead
Ford, Beverly Buren		Newstead
Ford, Hezekiah	before 1840	Goshen
Ford, Hezekiah	1846	Woodlawn/Cooper
Ford, Hezekiah	1858	Woodlawn/Cooper
Ford, Hezekiah - after 1850		Woodlawn/Cooper Cemetery - burial

Owner	Year	Subject
Ford, Hezekiah & Co	1814	Felixville
Ford, Mrs Annie M	1919	Rocky Mount
Ford, Mrs B B	1930	Newstead
Ford, Newton	1814	Felixville
Ford, Sterling	1814	Felixville
Foster, Courtney C	1872	Foster Place (Old)/Hobson Place
Foster, John T	1872	Liberty Hall
Foster, Mr & Mrs John T		Foster Graveyard (Old) - burial
Foster, Mr & Mrs Peter B Sr		Foster Graveyard (Old) - burial
Foster, Mrs Peter B		Liberty Hall
Foster, Peter		Effingham House
Foster, Peter B	1834	Burleigh Hall
Foster, Peter B before 1816		Cumberland Courthouse
Foster, Peter B - Tavern-Keeper	1829	Effingham House
Foster, Peter B	1831	Foster Graveyard (Old)
Foster, Peter B	1831	Langhorne's Tavern
Foster, Peter B	1831	Liberty Hall
Foster, Peter B	1831	Midway/Langhorne's Home
Foster, Peter B - grandchildren	by 1937	Foster Graveyard (Old)
Foster, Peter B Jr		Foster Graveyard (Old) - burial
Foster, Peter B Jr		Foster Place (Old)/Hobson Place
Foster, Peter B Sr	1831	Foster Place (Old)/Hobson Place
Foster, Samuel C	1931	Foster Place (Old)/Hobson Place
Foster, Thornton & Fannie	by 1938	Liberty Hall
Fowlkes, Joseph M	1873	Willow Bank/Isbell
Francisco, Peter	ca 1788	Locust Grove/Francisco
Frank, Rev & Mrs Luther B	1934	Mountain View/Locust Level
Franklin, B S & Lee	1928	Farmview
Franklin, S C	1920	Farmview
Fraser, James H	1902	Broomfield/Steger's Farm
Frayser, Dr Benjamin F - 1819-1852		Deanery Cemetery - inscription

Owner	Year	Subject
Frayser, Elizabeth Deane - 1848-1849		Deanery Cemetery - inscription
Frayser, Ellen - 1850-1852		Deanery Cemetery - inscription
Frayser, John	1814	Felixville
Frayser, William A	1835	Frayser's Tavern
Frayser, William A	1845	Frayser's Tavern
Fraysier, Narcissa M - 1847-1896		Johnson's Cemetery - inscription
Freese, Henry T	1913	Trenton/Brick House
Funkhouser, Amos P	1909	Oakland/Carrington
Funkhouser, Lucy (Carnes)	1921	Broomfield/Steger's Farm
Fuqua, Joseph	1855	Midway/Langhorne's Home
Fuqua, Joseph	1827	Stony Point/Stony Mill Site
Fuqua, Joseph & Ann	1831	Farmview
Furr, J M	1920	Burleigh Hall
Gaines, Bernard	1811	Booker's Mill
Gaines, Bernard - Tavern-Keeper	1777	Effingham House
Garnett, John E - 1860-1877		Locust Grove Cemetery - inscription
Garnett, George King	1918	Clare Farm/PowersPlace
Garnett, John C	1910	High Hill
Garnett, Mattie	1881	High Hill
Garnett, Robert S - 1821-1898		Locust Grove Cemetery - inscription
Garnett, Sara W - 1830-1890		Locust Grove Cemetery - inscription
Garret, J Wesley	before 1876	Melrose
Garrett, R C	1918	Effingham House
Garrett, Samuel	before 1855	Scott Home/Flippen Home
Garvin, J B	1906	Oak Hill
Gary, John A	1899	Locust Hill/Mayo
Gary, Mildred	1913	Locust Hill/Mayo
Gauldin, Josiah	1878	Locust Hill/Palmore
Gay, Bettie C	1887	Bonbrook
Germaine, E A	1915	Oak Hill
Gholson, Samuel Creed		Needham
Gibson, George A B	1843	Overton Home (Old)
Gibson, John T	1853	Overton Home (Old)
Gibson, Robert & Arabella	1802	Overton Home (Old)

Owner	Year	Subject
Gilbert, N H	1919	Gray Home
Giles, Elizabeth	1935	Refuge
Gilliam, Carter M - legatee	before 1852	Rose Cottage
Gilliam, Charles W	1857	Rose Hill
Gilliam, Edward	1876	Auburn
Gilliam, Edward	1859	Barter Hill
Gilliam, Miss Gay	1936	Barter Hill
Gilliam, Miss Gay		Barter Hill - inscription
Gilliam, V A		Barter Hill
Glen, Nathan - vestryman	1772	Glebe, The - Church of England
Glover, James H	1835	Forkland
Glover, Robert B	1835	Forkland
Godsey, A E Jr	1935	Burleigh Hall
Goodman, Charlie	1932	Frayser's Tavern
Goodman, Herbert	by 1937	Oatland
Goodman, Jack	1814	Felixville
Goodman, John W	1879	Oatland
Goodman, Joseph N - trustee	1856	Fork of Willis Church
Goodman, Joseph N	1841	Woodlawn/Ross
Goodman, Norton - trustee	1811	Felixville
Goodman, Robert I	1834	Rock Castle
Goodman, Robert T	1863	Gravel Hill
Goodman, Thomas B	1843	Woodbourne/Beech Run
Goodman, William I & Pocahontas V	1904	Willow Bank/Isbell
Goodman, Wilson N	before 1843	Woodbourne/Beech Run
Goodman, Zachariah - trustee	1811	Felixville
Goodman, Zachariah (whole town 1818-1823)	1818	Felixville
Goodman, Zachariah T	1853	Oatland
Gordon, Thomas - trustee	1811	Felixville
Gray, Andrew J	1876	Northfield
Gray, B H	1900	Trenton/Brick House
Gray, Herbert	before 1876	Melrose
Gray, James T	1876	Melrose
Gray, John Springer	by 1936	Northfield
Gray, Mr & Mrs	1936	Northfield Cemetery
Gray, Mrs Ida Scott	1891	Gray Home
Gray, Taylor	1910	Clay Bank
Gray, William		Northfield

Owner   Year   Subject

Gray, William	1750	Trenton Mill/Sport's Lake
Grigg, James A	1867	Briarfield
Grigg, Sarah R	after 1867	Briarfield
Grigg, Sarah R - heirs	1937	Briarfield
Haas, Charles	ca 1867	Effingham House
Haddix, Glen & Alexus	by 1996	Pleasant Grove
Haggeman	1907	Springfield
Haines, Travis	1936	Viewmont
Hamby, William & Judith	before 1820	Palmer's Tavern
Harlan, Mrs Max B Sr	1935	Tar Wallet Church
Harris, Allen H	1814	Felixville
Harris, Charlotte Anne - 1854-1857		Bonbrook Cemetery - inscription
Harris, John Lovell - 1848-1857		Bonbrook Cemetery - inscription
Harris, Joseph	1779	Oatland
Harris, Wallace Deane - 1857-1857		Bonbrook Cemetery - inscription
Harrison Family	by 1800	Clifton Cemetery
Harrison, Archibald M - 1794-1842		Clifton Cemetery - inscription
Harrison, Benjamin (....-1761)	before 1761	Englewood/Horn Quarter
Harrison, Benjamin (ca 1695-1745) - wife Anne Carter	before 1743	Glentivar
Harrison, Carter H - 1792-1843		Clifton Cemetery - inscription
Harrison, Carter Henry	1818	Glentivar
Harrison, Carter Henry - 1776-1800		Clifton Cemetery - inscription
Harrison, Carter Henry (1726 - 1794)	after 1745	Clifton/Harrison
Harrison, Carter Henry (1726-1794)	before 1788	Ampthill
Harrison, Carter Henry (1726-1794)	1745	Glentivar
Harrison, Cary	1761	Englewood/Horn Quarter
Harrison, Charles W	1917	Needham
Harrison, Col Randolph (1829-1900)	1858	Ampthill

Owner	Year	Subject
Harrison, Col Randolph - 1829-1900		Clifton Cemetery - inscription
Harrison, Dr Edward J	1854	Woodbourne/Beech Run
Harrison, Dr Edward J - heirs	1903	Woodbourne/Beech Run
Harrison, Edmund	1808	Mill Mount
Harrison, Edmund	1808	Stony Point/Stony Mill Site
Harrison, Edmund (1764-1828)	before 1814	Hors du Monde
Harrison, Edward Jacquelin - 1824-1903		Clifton Cemetery - inscription
Harrison, Eliza	1837	Morven
Harrison, George F (1821-....)		Elkora/Walnut Hill
Harrison, Henningham Carrington (Wills) - 1801-1864		Clifton Cemetery - inscription
Harrison, Jane Cary (Carr) - 1807-1859		Clifton Cemetery - inscription
Harrison, Janetta R		Glentivar
Harrison, Kitty (Heth) - 1800-1833		Clifton Cemetery - inscription
Harrison, Lula	1926	Reynolds Home
Harrison, Major Carter H heirs	after 1861	Elkora/Walnut Hill
Harrison, Major Carter Henry (1831-1861)	1855	Elkora/Walnut Hill
Harrison, Mary (Randolph) - 1773-1835		Clifton Cemetery - inscription
Harrison, Mary L (Harrison) Mrs E C	by 1936	Elkora/Walnut Hill
Harrison, Mrs E J	1922	Morningside
Harrison, Mrs Harriet (Heillman)	1908	Ampthill
Harrison, Nelson Page - 1855-1855		Clifton Cemetery - inscription
Harrison, Peyton	1845	Glentivar
Harrison, Peyton - 1800-1887		Clifton Cemetery - inscription
Harrison, Randolph (1769-1839)	1835	Ampthill
Harrison, Randolph (1769-1839)	after 1794	Clifton/Harrison
Harrison, Randolph (1769-1839)	before 1820	Morven

Owner	Year	Subject
Harrison, Randolph	1790	Glentivar
Harrison, Randolph - 1769-1839		Clifton Cemetery - inscription
Harrison, Randolph - 1798-1844		Clifton Cemetery - inscription
Harrison, Rev Peyton (1800-1887)	after 1859	Clifton/Harrison
Harrison, Robert Carter (1765-) after 1788		Ampthill
Harrison, Sally H (Browne) - 1825-1849		Clifton Cemetery - inscription
Harrison, Thomas Randolph - 1791-1833		Clifton Cemetery - inscription
Harrison, Virginia Randolph - 1834-1850		Clifton Cemetery - inscription
Harrison, William B (1800-1870)	1843	Ampthill
Harrison, Wm Byrd - 1837-1846		Clifton Cemetery - inscription
Hartsook, Daniel & Elizabeth	1838	Cedar Plains
Hartsook, Elizabeth (Carrington)	before 1841	Solitude
Harvey, C C	1921	Ca Ira Mill
Hatcher, Frederick - vestryman	1772	Glebe, The - Church of England
Hatcher, M F	1920	Boston Hill
Hatcher, Maria (Carrington) - 1795-1857		Oakland/Carrington - inscription
Hatcher, R S	1929	Boston Hill
Hatcher, Samuel - trustee	1846	Thomas Chapel
Hawkins, Amelia M	1870	Woodville Site
Hawkins, Hannah B	1870	Woodville Site
Hawkins, J L	1870	Woodville Site
Hazelgrove, Joseph W	1898	Forkland
Hazelgrove, Joseph W - heirs	by 1937	Forkland
Hazlegrove, Charles et al		Willow Bank/McGehee
Hazlegrove, Winston	1848	Willow Bank/McGehee
Henderson, Dr Robert	about 1817	Northfield
Henderson, Mrs Louisa - 1802-1870		Northfield Cemetery - inscription
Henderson, Robert	1848	Forkland

Owner	Year	Subject
Henderson, Robert, M. D. - 1795-1862		Northfield Cemetery - inscription
Henderson, W F	1912	Burleigh Hall
Hendrick, David	1832	Locust Grove/Hendrick Home/Allen Home
Hendrick, Mathew	before 1832	Locust Grove/Hendrick Home/Allen Home
Hendricks, David & Eliza	1832	Hendrick Home (Old)
Hendricks, Matthew & Frances	before 1832	Hendrick Home (Old)
Hobson, Adcock - vestryman	1772	Glebe, The - Church of England
Hobson, Benjamin	1841	Frayser's Tavern
Hobson, Epa	before 1835	Frayser's Tavern
Hobson, James - trustee	1847	Center Presbyterian Church
Hobson, Maurice	1819	Booker's Mill
Hobson, Maurice L	1828	Booker's Mill
Hobson, Maurice L	1829	Booker's Mill
Hobson, Maurice Langhorne - Tavern-Keeper	1824	Effingham House
Hobson, Rosa V	before 1931	Foster Place (Old)/Hobson Place
Hobson, Samuel	ca 1840	Effingham House
Hobson, Samuel & Maria	before 1847	Center Presbyterian Church
Hobson, Thomas	1819	Booker's Mill
Hobson, Thomas	1807	Effingham House
Hobson, Thomas - Tavern-Keeper	1802	Effingham House
Hobson, William B	1829	Burleigh Hall
Hobson, William B - Tavern-Keeper	1833	Effingham House
Hodgson, George P	1911	Solitude
Hodgson, Martha P	1897	Solitude
Holeman, John	1807	Corson Home/Coupland's Tavern
Holman, H S	by 1936	Greenwood
Holman, John	before 1855	Cherry Grove/Sanderson Home
Holman, John	by 1937	Holman Place (Old)
Holman, John	before 1851	Holman Place (Old)
Holman, Nathan G	1918	Cherry Grove/Sanderson Home

Owner	Year	Subject
Holman, Nathan G		Holman Place (Old)
Holman, William	1855	Cherry Grove/Sanderson Home
Holman, William		Greenwood
Holman, William	1851	Holman Place (Old)
Hooe, Peter H	1863	Rocky Mount
Horan, Thomas	1932	Langhorne's Tavern
Howard, Alfred F	1916	Needham
Howard, Alfred F	1918	Needham
Howard, Mary E & A F	1914	Needham
Hubbard, Bolling et al	before 1876	Glen Mary
Hubbard, Edmund W	1846	Glen Mary
Hubbard, Philip A	1876	Glen Mary
Hudgins, E A & wife Emily		Austin Home
Hudgins, Elizabeth M - legatee	before 1852	Rose Cottage
Hudgins, H H	1931	Oakland/Carrington
Hudgins, Henry C & wife Mary (Austin)		Austin Home
Hudgins, Henry V - executor		Hudgins Tavern/Locust Grove
Hudgins, John	by 1815	Hudgins Tavern/Locust Grove
Hudgins, John A - legatee	before 1852	Rose Cottage
Hudgins, Marion A	1882	Austin Home
Hudgins, Robert & wife Narcissus (Austin)		Austin Home
Hudgins, Robert S	1873	Scott Home/Flippen Home
Hughes family		Muddy Creek Mill/Moon's Mill
Hughes, Edward	1821	Cherry Grove/Thweatt
Hughes, Edward Jr		Pine Forest/Hughes Place
Hughes, Edward Sr	before 1855	Pine Forest/Hughes Place
Hughes, James	by 1937	Pine Forest/Hughes Place
Hughes, John	1819	Cherry Grove/Thweatt
Hughes, John	1832	Hickory Hall
Hughes, John	before 1811	White Level
Hughes, John	before 1847	Gray Home
Hughes, John & Mary	1845	Meador's Store/Old Store
Hughes, John Woodfin - 1831-1898		Guinea Church Cemetery - inscription

Owner	Year	Subject
Hughes, Martha H - 1831-1908		Guinea Church Cemetery - inscription
Hughes, Mary Venable	1909	Peaceful Level
Hughes, Thomas W		Willow Bank/McGehee
Hughes, William Blanton - - 1916		Guinea Church Cemetery - inscription
Irving, Ann Mildred - 1820-1820		Deanery Cemetery - inscription
Irving, Elizabeth H (Deane) - 1803-1833		Deanery Cemetery - inscription
Irving, F D		Deanery Cemetery
Irving, F D	by 1936	Deanery, The
Irving, Frances D		
- wife Lucy Cushing	before 1874	Fork, The
Irving, Francis Arianna - 1853-1854		Deanery Cemetery - inscription
Irving, Lucy (Cushing) - 1830-1855		Fork Cemetery - inscription
Irving, Paulus A E, M D - 1831-1853		Deanery Cemetery - inscription
Irving, Robert - 1790-1850		Deanery Cemetery - inscription
Irving, Robert - 1850-1853		Fork Cemetery - inscription
Irving, Robert T - 1836-1838		Deanery Cemetery - inscription
Irwin, Mary B	1863	Irwin's Tavern Site
Irwin, William	before 1833	Irwin's Tavern Site
Isbell, James	1830	Willow Bank/Isbell
Isbell, James D	1848	Willow Bank/Isbell
Isbell, Lewis - heirs	before 1830	Forkland
Isbell, Lewis	1811	Willow Bank/Isbell
Isbell, Lewis	1812	Woodlawn/Epps
Isbell, Lewis M & Eliza A	1827	Woodlawn/Epps
Isbell, Thomas M & Frances A	1849	Willow Bank/Isbell
Jackson, Benjamin F		Gravel Hill
Jackson, Elisha	1846	Hooper's Rock
Jackson, Elisha, Elvira, & B F	1866	Hooper's Rock
Jackson, Peter	1842	Trenton Mill/Sport's Lake
Jacques, Susie	1897	Englewood/Horn Quarter
James, Francis H		
- Tavern-Keeper	1837	Effingham House

Owner	Year	Subject
James, Frederick J	1802	Muddy Creek Mill/Moon's Mill
Jarrett, D L	1919	Willow Bank/Isbell
Jarrett, Mr & Mrs Wm P	1926	Willow Bank/Isbell
Jarrett, Thomas W	1926	Willow Bank/Isbell
Jenkins, Rev Joseph Hull	ca 1817	Cumberland Baptist Church/Jenkins Church
Jeter, Allen - trustee	1811	Felixville
Jeter, Rhodophil - trustee	1811	Felixville
Johns, James	before 1831	Briarfield
Johns, Joseph	before 1832	Flippen Home
Johns, Joseph	before 1780	Guinea Mills
Johns, Robert T	1859	Briarfield
Johns, Robert T	before 1859	Guinea Mills
Johns, Thomas	before 1780	Guinea Mills
Johnson, A Martin	1933	Trenton Mill/Sport's Lake
Johnson, Alexander - 1804-1878		Johnson's Cemetery - inscription
Johnson, Ann (Mrs Littleton)	1871	Rosebank
Johnson, Archibald & Harriet	before 1820	Palmer's Tavern
Johnson, Benjamin	1820	Palmer's Tavern
Johnson, David & Susan	1848	Trenton Mill/Sport's Lake
Johnson, Eliza	1832	Rose Hill
Johnson, Hugh - 1832-1908		Guinea Church Cemetery - inscription
Johnson, Judith	1832	Rose Hill
Johnson, Littleton T	1868	Rosebank
Johnson, Louisa (Henderson) - 1848-1916		Guinea Church Cemetery - inscription
Johnson, Lucy Nelson (Page) - 1852-1895		Guinea Church Cemetery - inscription
Johnson, Martha	1832	Rose Hill
Johnson, Martha - 1823-1859		Johnson's Cemetery - inscription
Johnson, Mary B - 1808-1864		Johnson's Cemetery - inscription
Johnson, Mrs Watkins	1832	Rose Hill
Johnson, Richard	1832	Rose Hill
Johnson, Sarah	1832	Rose Hill
Johnson, Thomas	1812	Rose Hill
Johnson, Thomas & Judith	before 1820	Palmer's Tavern

Owner	Year	Subject
Johnson, Watkins	1816	Rose Hill
Johnson, Watkins	1832	Rose Hill
Johnson, William B	1863	Rosebank
Jones, John H	before 1848	Hickory Hill/Hard Bargain
Jones, P R	1936	Cedar Grove/Bryant Place
Jones, Powhatan - trustee	1847	Center Presbyterian Church
Jones, Rebecca E	1878	Walnut Hill
Jones, Robert	1819	Booker's Mill
Keeble, Walter & Sally	1804	Woodlawn/Epps
Keeling, George	before 1795	Ca Ira Mill
Keller, D A	1901	Trent's Mill
Kinckle, Maria W (Page)	after 1877	Union Hill
King, John P	1840	Dawson Home
King, R W	1934	Englewood/Horn Quarter
Kirkpatrick, Arianna Deane -	1855-1861	Deanery Cemetery - inscription
Kirkpatrick, Rev John	1819	Clifton/Meadors
Lamb, J F & Nannie Clee	1937	Goshen
Lancaster Family	ca 1742	Rochelle
Lancaster, Fannie V	1867	Englewood/Horn Quarter
Lancaster, J P (son)		Walnut Hill
Lancaster, Mrs E P & Mr & Mrs Preston	by 1997	Rochelle
Lancaster, Mrs Edwin P	1942	Rochelle
Lancaster, Rev James L	1893	Rochelle
Lancaster, Susan G (Mrs Wm L)		Walnut Hill
Lancaster, William	1863	Englewood/Horn Quarter
Lancaster, William	1911	Hickory Hill/Hard Bargain
Lancaster, William & Mary E	1909	Trenton/Brick House
Lancaster, William L	1882	Walnut Hill
Lancaster, William LeGrand	1924	Rochelle
Langhorne, Maurice - Tavern-Keeper	1789	Effingham House
Langhorne, Maurice	before 1831	Foster Place (Old)/Hobson Place
Langhorne, Maurice	before 1767	Langhorne's Tavern
Langhorne, Maurice - vestryman	1772	Glebe, The - Church of England
Langhorne, Maurice & Elizabeth	before 1831	Liberty Hall

Owner	Year	Subject
Langhorne, Maurice (1721-1791)	before 1775	Effingham House
Langhorne, Maurice Jr	1813	Foster Graveyard (Old)
Langhorne, Maurice Jr	1812	Langhorne's Tavern
Langhorne, Maurice Jr	1823	Langhorne's Tavern
Langhorne, Maurice Jr	1812	Midway/Langhorne's Home
Langhorne, Maurice Jr	1821	Midway/Langhorne's Home
Langhorne, Maurice Jr	1824	Stony Point/Stony Mill Site
Langhorne, William Beverly	after 1791	Effingham House
Langhorne, William Beverly - Tavern-Keeper	1800	Effingham House
Lawford, Thomas W	1888	Bonbrook
Leach, J H C	1832	Rochelle
Leach, James P		Rochelle
Leard, Ellsworth	1915	Hickory Hill/Hard Bargain
Lee, James D	before 1845	Millview
Lee, James D - heirs	before 1845	Millview
Lee, Joseph D	1830	Ashland
Lee, William	1839	Womack Place (Old)
Lewis, Benjamin	1835	Woodlawn/Ross
Lewis, Gilley	before 1796	Rocky Mount
Ligon, C C	by 1937	Ashland
Ligon, Daniel	1824	Guinea Church/Tuggle's Meeting House
Ligon, I G	by 1937	Ashland
Ligon, Mrs Anderson (McGehee)		Ashland
Ligon, W V	by 1937	Ashland
Lipscomb, Henry	before 1778	Southall
Littleton Parish Vestrymen	after 1774	Browns Presbyterian Church
Logan, Lloyd	1863	Midway/Langhorne's Home
Logan, Lloyd	1863	Mountain View/Locust Level
Loveing, Seaton H	1873	Woodlawn/Ross
Lowman, Fannie A	1894	Underhill Site
Macon, Henry	1752	Popepand/Swann Place
Macon, John	1783	Rose Hill
Macon, Mrs Henry	1783	Popepand/Swann Place
Macon, Sallie	1797	Popepand/Swann Place
Macon, William	before 1752	Popepand/Swann Place
Macon, William	1797	Popepand/Swann Place

Owner	Year	Subject
Maddox, Thomas - trustee	1846	Thomas Chapel
Maddox, William	before 1779	Oatland
Maddox, William G	before 1840	Thomas Chapel
Maham, Harriet	1926	Reynolds Home
Manson, Polly	1870	High Hill
Marshall, H H	before 1857	Thackston Home (Old)
Martin, John	1935	Reynolds Home
Martin, John M	1920	Melrose
Matthews & Montague - trustees	before 1873	Blanton Home (Old)
Matthews, George	1850	Ca Ira Mill
Mayo family		Hooper's Rock
Mayo, Daniel	before 1796	Broomfield/Steger's Farm
Mayo, Edward C	1851	Locust Hill/Mayo
Mayo, George	1811	Hooper's Rock
Mayo, Joseph	before 1811	Hooper's Rock
Mayo, Joseph	before 1797	Solitude
Mayo, Thomas T	1813	Hooper's Rock
Mayo, William	before 1851	Locust Hill/Mayo
Mayo, William H	1839	Boston Hill
Mayo, William H	1851	Locust Hill/Mayo
McAshan, John T	1836	Trenton Mill/Sport's Lake
McAshan, William L	1836	Ca Ira Mill
McClellan, Dr & Mrs James	1983	Goshen
McCrum, J W	1918	Gray Home
McCullough, William's wife -	1808-1841	McCullough Tombstone - inscription
McGehee, John B	1859	Briarfield
McGehee, John B	1859	Guinea Mills
McGehee, Sarah (Woodfin)	after 1855	Ashland
McGehee, Thomas B	before 1848	Willow Bank/McGehee
McGehee, Thomas B & Lucy Ann	1848	Woodlawn/Epps
McRae, Donald	1906	Mountain View/Locust Level
McRae, Donald	1919	Willow Bank/Isbell
McRae, Mrs Emily	1865	Mountain View/Locust Level
McRae, Paul	1906	Mountain View/Locust Level

Owner	Year	Subject
McRae, Rev Christopher - minister, Church of England	1773	Glebe, The
Meador, H J	1892	Buena Vista Site
Meador, H J	1892	Meador's Store/Old Store
Meador, John	1902	Bookers Tavern
Meador, Leake S	1881	Mountain View/Meador Place
Meador, Mrs E R	1926	Buena Vista Site
Meador, Mrs H J	1926	Buena Vista Site
Meadors, John	before 1819	Clifton/Meadors
Meinhard, Amelia M	1925	Clare Farm/PowersPlace
Meredith, Bettie (Cushing) - 1831-1865		Fork Cemetery - inscription
Meredith, William		Raines Tavern/Wright's Ordinary
Mering, Mrs Myrtle Phillips	1937	Willow Bank/Isbell
Messinger, A E	1922	Oakland/Carrington
Mettauer, Joseph	before 1802	Overton Home (Old)
Metts, Dr & Mrs J C Jr	before 1993	Clifton/Harrison
Metts, Dr & Mrs Julian C Jr	before 1993	Clifton Cemetery
Meyers, David	1882	Dawson Home
Miller, Capt John		Cottage Grove Cemetery - no marker
Miller, Dr John T		Cottage Grove Cemetery - no marker
Miller, Giles A & Martha S	1862	Woodlawn/Epps
Miller, J F & wife	1886	Underhill Site
Miller, James	after 1865	Clifton/Harrison
Miller, James & Virginia	1849	White Level
Miller, John	before 1825	Locust Grove Cemetery
Miller, John	1825	Locust Grove/Nelson
Miller, John	1805	Talley Home
Miller, John	1817	Cottage Grove
Miller, John - founder	1825	Guinea Church/Tuggle's Meeting House
Miller, John & Martha	before 1836	High Hill
Miller, John T	1855	Cottage Grove
Miller, John T	1851	Midway/Langhorne's Home
Miller, Martha Todd - 1785-1850		Cottage Grove Cemetery - inscription
Miller, Sam	by 1937	Cottage Grove
Miller, William M	before 1845	Pine Forest/Hughes Place

Owner	Year	Subject
Mills, W R	1912	Woodlawn/Ross
Minor, John	1830	Refuge
Minter family	about 1800	Minter Site
Mitchell, Cary	before 1820	Morven
Mitchell, Cary	1811	White Level
Montague, Annie K	1916	Effingham House
Montague, J W		Solitude
Montague, William	1810	Cedar Plains
Moon family	1888	Muddy Creek Mill/Moon's Mill
Moon, A F		Muddy Creek Mill/Moon's Mill
Morgan, Dan	1785	Muddy Creek Mill/Moon's Mill
Morrison, W F	1892	Burleigh Hall
Morton, R C	1891	Meador's Store/Old Store
Morton, R G	1891	Buena Vista Site
Morton, W S	1836	High Hill
Mosby, Victoria G		Hooper's Rock
Mosby, William G & Amelia	1849	Willow Bank/Isbell
Moseley, Mrs Trent	1880	Springfield
Moseley, Trent	1888	Springfield
Moses, Julia L	1903	Trenton/Brick House
Nash, Abner	1831	Morven
Nash, Thomas	ca 1811	Rock Castle
Nash, Thomas - 1782-1813		Rock Castle - burial
Nash, Thomas P	1813	Rock Castle
Nelson, Andrew	1822	Locust Grove/Nelson
Nelson, Dr R E		Cobham
Nelson, John J		Cobham
Nelson, Judge William	ca 1836	Cobham
Nelson, Mrs John J	ca 1937	Cobham
New, Elizabeth R	1899	Mountain View/Locust Level
Noel, John & Mary	1845	Walton's Mill
Nuckols, M W	1919	Englewood/Horn Quarter
Oliver, Bettie - Bryant/Oliver, heirs		Cedar Grove/Bryant Place
Oliver, James - Bryant/Oliver, heirs		Cedar Grove/Bryant Place
Oliver, W Edgar	1901	Cedar Grove/Bryant Place
Owenby family of Tennessee	by 1936	Felixville
Owenby, Pearl	1932	Farmview

Owner	Year	Subject
Ownby	before 1969	Auburn
Page family		Union Hill Cemetery
Page Family		Fork Cemetery
Page Family		Minter Site
Page, Alexander T - 1819-1845		Northfield Cemetery - inscription
Page, Archibald	1853	Auburn
Page, Archibald Cary - 1824-1871		Union Hill Cemetery - inscription
Page, Eliza Trent - 1815-1838		Union Hill Cemetery - inscription
Page, Ellen Cary - 1817-1837		Union Hill Cemetery - inscription
Page, Harriet R	after 1877	Union Hill
Page, John C	1857	Auburn
Page, John C		Union Hill
Page, John C - 1784-1853		Union Hill Cemetery - inscription
Page, John C & Mary Anne (Trent)	after 1808	Trent's Mill
Page, Joseph	1936	Peabody Place (Old)
Page, Julia R (Trent) Gray	1884	Clay Bank
Page, Lt Col John C - CSA		Clay Bank - graveyard
Page, Lucia Cary (Harrison) - 1809-1842		Fork Cemetery - inscription
Page, Lucy A (Trent) - 1826-1853		Union Hill Cemetery - inscription
Page, Major Carter (1759-1825)	1782	Fork, The
Page, Martha	1900	Peabody Place (Old)
Page, Mary A (Trent)	about 1853	Union Hill
Page, Mrs Martha (Henderson) - 1821-1842		Northfield Cemetery - inscription
Page, Nelson	1829	Englewood/Horn Quarter
Page, Nelson - 1801-1850		Fork Cemetery - inscription
Page, Nelson (1801-1850)	after 1825	Fork, The
Page, Reynolds & A C	1867	Trent's Mill
Page, Robert Burwell - 1806-1837		Fork Cemetery - inscription
Page, William N	1836	Midway/Langhorne's Home
Page, William N Jr - 1841-1861		Fork Cemetery - inscription
Page, William N - trustee	1847	Center Presbyterian Church
Page, William Nelson	1830	Englewood/Horn Quarter

Owner	Year	Subject
Painter, Alfred M	1874	Rocky Mount
Palmer, John F	1854	Palmer's Tavern
Palmer, Mr & Mrs Bennett W	by 1936	Palmer's Tavern
Palmore, Charles B	1878	Locust Hill/Palmore
Palmore, Charles B Jr	by 1937	Locust Hill/Palmore
Palmore, Charles S	before 1840	Clare Farm/PowersPlace
Palmore, Charles S	before 1840	Dunleith
Palmore, Charles S - Tavern-Keeper	1842	Effingham House
Palmore, Charles S	1827	Stony Point/Stony Mill Site
Palmore, E R	1887	Stony Point/Stony Mill Site
Palmore, George W	1872	Buena Vista Site
Palmore, George W		Chow Chow /Phillips Home
Palmore, George W	1872	Meador's Store/Old Store
Palmore, James Watson	by 1937	Locust Hill/Palmore
Palmore, John F	1848	Refuge
Palmore, John R	1824	Stony Point/Stony Mill Site
Palmore, Joseph - legatee	before 1852	Rose Cottage
Palmore, Joseph L	1800	Locust Hill/Palmore
Palmore, Joseph S	1843	Midway/Langhorne's Home
Palmore, Joseph S - 1805-1846		Palmore Cemetery - inscription
Palmore, Martha J	1897	Locust Hill/Palmore
Palmore, Mr	1871	Ca Ira Mill
Parker, Early	by 1936	Southall
Parker, Holland	1894	Englewood/Horn Quarter
Parker, Isham	1870	Scott Home/Flippen Home
Parker, Isham & Ann Lou	1884	Southall
Parker, Spencer W	1911	Irwin's Tavern Site
Parrack, Segul H	1842	Smith Place (Old)
Parrack, Thomas	1852	Smith Place (Old)
Parrish, Alonza J	1884	Oakland/Carrington
Parrish, H T	1921	Goshen
Parrish, Thomas J	after 1865	Oakland/Carrington
Parrish, Valentine - trustee	1847	Center Presbyterian Church
Payne, Dr Thomas E	1935	Mill Mount
Peabody, D C	1877	Peabody Place (Old)
Peace, S T	1919	Rochelle
Peace, Willie P	1937	Rochelle
Peasley, Gabriel B	1846	Gravel Hill
Perkins et al	before 1846	Glen Mary

Owner	Year	Subject
Perkins, Ann J	1862	Forkland
Perkins, Baby - -1863		Northfield Cemetery - inscription
Perkins, Fannie Archer - 1859-1862		Northfield Cemetery - inscription
Perkins, Jesse - trustee	1856	Fork of Willis Church
Perkins, Judge William A - 1817-1889		Northfield Cemetery - inscription
Perkins, Mrs Anna J - 1823-1894		Northfield Cemetery - inscription
Perkins, Robert Henderson - 1853-1854		Northfield Cemetery - inscription
Perkins, Sarah Price (Gilliam)	1888	Auburn
Perkins, William Allan - 1861-1862		Northfield Cemetery - inscription
Peters, B A	1927	Langhorne's Tavern
Peters, Sally		Hooper's Rock
Pettus, Hugh M	1841	Burleigh Hall
Phillippi, John	1908	Locust Grove/Flippen
Phillips, Elizabeth (widow)	1851	Chow Chow /Phillips Home
Phillips, Malcolm & Cecil	1913	Trenton Mill/Sport's Lake
Phillips, Mrs Fannie Myrtle	1926	Willow Bank/Isbell
Phillips, Peter	ca 1832	Chow Chow /Phillips Home
Piedmont Lumber Co	1915	Union Hill
Piercy, A N	1917	Hudgins Tavern/Locust Grove
Pittman, Henningham (Carrington)	ca 1808	Walton's Mill
Porter, Ada - Bryant/Oliver, heirs		Cedar Grove/Bryant Place
Powell, Benjamin H		Muddy Creek Mill/Moon's Mill
Powell, Nathaniel & Sophonisba	1838	Cedar Plains
Powell, Sophinisba (Carrington)	before 1842	Solitude
Powell, William - trustee	1811	Felixville
Power, Thomas		Chow Chow /Phillips Home
Powers, S B	before 1892	Dunleith
Powers, Spencer B	1869	Clare Farm/PowersPlace
Powers, T Hyde	1904	Clare Farm/PowersPlace
Powers, Thomas M	1840	Clare Farm/PowersPlace
Powers, Thomas M	1840	Dunleith

Owner	Year	Subject
Price, Fannie P	1870	High Hill
Price, J J	by 1936	Raines Tavern/Wright's Ordinary
Pruden, Addie E (Carnes)	1921	Broomfield/Steger's Farm
Putney, Fred W	by 1998	Thackston Home (Old)
Putney, Rosa I & her husband		Trenton Mill/Sport's Lake
Putney, S W	1918	Rochelle
Putney, Walter G	by 1998	Thackston Home (Old)
Raine, John	1806	Raines Tavern/Wright's Ordinary
Randall, Mrs Jane (Harrison)	1870	Ampthill
Randolph family	before 1781	Bizarre
Randolph, Beverly	before 1915	Union Hill
Randolph, D Coupland & Harriet (Page)		Union Hill
Randolph, D Coupland Jr	before 1915	Union Hill
Randolph, Dr John	1890	Glentivar
Randolph, Isham & Nancy	before 1798	Clay Bank
Randolph, Isham - 1771-1844		Clifton Cemetery - inscription
Randolph, John	1796-1810	Bizarre
Randolph, Judith	1813	Bizarre
Randolph, Mary A	before 1915	Union Hill
Randolph, Richard & Judith	1790	Bizarre
Randolph, Thomas	before 1723	Glentivar
Randolph, Thomas	before 1796	Clay Bank
Randolph, Thomas Jr & Mary	before 1798	Clay Bank
Randolph, William & Jane	1820	Morven
Ransom, William	1854	Chow Chow /Phillips Home
Reid, Manus	1919	Overton Home (Old)
Resettlement Administration	ca 1936	Oak Hill
Resettlement Administration	1936	Trenton/Brick House
Reynolds, John O	1868	Reynolds Home
Reynolds, John O	1887	Woodside Site
Rhodes, W H		Muddy Creek Mill/Moon's Mill
Richardson, E L	1937	Spring Hill/Cook's Tract
Richardson, John H & Mary A	1819	Langhorne's Tavern
Richardson, Richard - heirs		Boston Hill
Richardson, Susannah - wife		Boston Hill
Roberts, Mr & Mrs	1926	Willow Bank/Isbell

Owner	Year	Subject
Robertson, John	1823	Hors du Monde
Robertson, Wyndham	1823	Hors du Monde
Robins, Dr Alexander		
Spotswood	1970	Goshen
Robinson, Alfred D	1848	Walton's Mill
Robinson, Edward	1763	Talley Home
Robinson, Eric L	before 1996	Spring Hill/Cook's Tract
Robinson, Jeffrey	1908	Talley Home
Robinson, John	1867	Effingham House
Robinson, John	before 1763	Talley Home
Robinson, John & Ann	1841	Trenton Mill/Sport's Lake
Robinson, John B	1848	Hickory Hill/Hard Bargain
Robinson, William B	1896	Hickory Hill/Hard Bargain
Rodgers, Mrs Kate	by 1936	Woodbourne/Beech Run
Rogers, J T	1924	Ampthill
Ross, David	ca 1774	Cobham
Ross, David		Cobham
Ross, David	before 1810	Woodlawn/Ross
Ross, Frederick	1834	Woodlawn/Ross
Ross, William		Cobham
Rowh, John D	1923	Oakland/Carrington
Rudd, W T	1903	Englewood/Horn Quarter
Russell, Ann	1858	Mountain View/Meador Place
Russell, Fannie & Richard	1858	Mountain View/Meador Place
Russell, Nancy	1814	Mountain View/Meador Place
Rutherford, Mary (Henderson) - 1824-1846		Northfield Cemetery - inscription
Rutherford, Robert H - 1844-1863		Northfield Cemetery - inscription
Sanderson, C R	1912	Reynolds Home
Sanderson, Daniel	1843	Rocky Mount
Sanderson, Fannie & Nannie		Locust Grove/Flippen
Sanderson, Fannie A	1918	Cherry Grove/Sanderson Home
Sanderson, Jane	1867	Locust Grove/Flippen
Sanderson, John	1821	Rocky Mount
Sanderson, Mrs C R	by 1936	Jesse Thomas Site
Sanderson, Obadiah - trustee	1846	Thomas Chapel

Owner	Year	Subject
Sanderson, Ollie	1937	Cherry Grove/Sanderson Home
Sanderson, Thomas B	1844	Woodbourne/Beech Run
Sanderson, Willie	1823	Rocky Mount
Satterwhite, S J	1919	Rochelle
Saunders, James & Dale	by 1993	Ampthill
Schomberg, Marion N	1912	Solitude
Schomberg, Marion N	1921	Solitude
Scott, Charles (1739-1813)		Scott's Hill
Scott, George	1901	Cedar Bluff/Scott Place
Scott, George O	1855	Hickory Hall
Scott, George O	1863	Mountain View/Locust Level
Scott, George O	1864	Mountain View/Locust Level
Scott, Joel J	1844	Hickory Hall
Scott, Joel J	1851	Woodlawn/Epps
Scott, Joseph	ca 1854	West Hill
Scott, Martha Ann	1872	Scott Home/Flippen Home
Scott, Richard M	1855	Scott Home/Flippen Home
Scott, Seymour - vestryman	1772	Glebe, The - Church of England
Scott, Thomas	1847	Gray Home
Scott, Thomas - heirs	before 1891	Gray Home
Scott, Thomas P	1936	Cedar Bluff/Scott Place
Scott, Thomas W	1855	Hickory Hall
Scott, William H	1860	Scott Home/Flippen Home
Scruggs, Edward P estate		Midway/Langhorne's Home
Scruggs, Edward	1798	Englewood/Horn Quarter
Scruggs, Edward L	1823	Englewood/Horn Quarter
Scruggs, Gutheridge P estate	1843	Midway/Langhorne's Home
Shelton, John M	1869	Woodlawn/Ross
Shelton, John M	1873	Woodlawn/Ross
Shepard, S W	1896	Dunleith
Shepard, Samuel	1807	Corson Home/Coupland's Tavern
Shepherd, J C	1907	Chow Chow /Phillips Home
Sheppener, Clement C	1877	Peabody Place (Old)
Sheppener, Mildred C	1843	Peabody Place (Old)
Shields, Alfred	1837	Mount Elba

Owner	Year	Subject
Shields, B P - 1820-		Mount Elba Cemetery - inscription
Shields, David W - 1816-1833		Mount Elba Cemetery - inscription
Shields, Dr Alfred W - 1807-1841		Mount Elba Cemetery - inscription
Shields, Henningham	1837	Mount Elba
Shields, John B - 1815-1818		Mount Elba Cemetery - inscription
Shields, Joseph	1837	Mount Elba
Shields, Judith	1837	Mount Elba
Shields, M J - 1821-		Mount Elba Cemetery - inscription
Shields, Major David	before 1837	Mount Elba
Shields, Major David - 1768-1837		Mount Elba Cemetery - inscription
Shields, Mary	1837	Mount Elba
Shields, Polly C	1837	Mount Elba
Shields, Thomas	1837	Mount Elba
Shields, Thomas P	1854	Mount Elba
Shields, Virginia	1837	Mount Elba
Shores, Sally Ann (Wood) - Mrs John Francis		Glentivar
Sims, Bernard	1814	Midway/Langhorne's Home
Sims, Col Reuben T	before 1840	Dawson Home
Sims, Edward	1850	Ca Ira Mill
Sims, Edward B	1850	Womack Place (Old)
Sims, Edward W	1821	Midway/Langhorne's Home
Skipwith, George N	1832	Hickory Hall
Skipwith, Henry	1778	Mill Mount
Skipwith, Mary	1832	Hickory Hall
Skipwith, William - trustee	1811	Felixville
Skipwith, William	1814	Hors du Monde
Skipwith, William	1801	Mill Mount
Skipwith, William	before 1808	Stony Point/Stony Mill Site
Smith, Alice A	1867	Midway/Langhorne's Home
Smith, Anna L	1867	Midway/Langhorne's Home
Smith, Arthur J	by 1937	Womack Place (Old)
Smith, Augustine I	1863	Woodlawn/Ross
Smith, Dr J W	1914	Clare Farm/PowersPlace
Smith, Dr J W	1925	Clare Farm/PowersPlace

Owner	Year	Subject
Smith, Dr J W	1911	Jiltic Farm/Booker's Mill
Smith, Dr Weldon J	1914	Hors du Monde
Smith, Fred W	1843	Clifton/Meadors
Smith, George E B	1899	Booker Cemetery (Old)
Smith, George E B	1899	Woodside Site
Smith, George E B - relatives		Booker Cemetery (Old)
Smith, H P	1917	Mill Mount
Smith, Henry		Greenwood
Smith, Henry	1845	White Level
Smith, J Spurgeon	1906	Smith Place (Old)
Smith, J W	1923	Clare Farm/PowersPlace
Smith, J Weldon	1913	Cherry Grove/Thweatt
Smith, J Weldon	1919	Clare Farm/PowersPlace
Smith, John M	1851	Womack Place (Old)
Smith, Judge William M	by 1937	Clare Farm/PowersPlace
Smith, L H	1911	Smith Place (Old)
Smith, Martha C	1867	Midway/Langhorne's Home
Smith, Martha S	1874	Mount Airy
Smith, Mary R	1911	Smith Place (Old)
Smith, Miss Hattie A	1907	Clifton/Meadors
Smith, Moses A	1852	Smith Place (Old)
Smith, Nannie B	1867	Midway/Langhorne's Home
Smith, Peter B	1905	Smith Place (Old)
Smith, Rev G E B - 1871-1915		Booker Cemetery (Old) - inscription
Smith, Robert	1785	Booker's Mill
Smith, Robert - Tavern-Keeper	1797	Effingham House
Smith, Robert	1810	Smith Place (Old)
Smith, Robert	before 1814	Smith's Chapel
Smith, S A	1859	Clifton/Meadors
Smith, William E	1850	Dawson Home
Smith, William E	1848	White Level
Smith, William James		Booker Cemetery (Old)
Smith, William M	1906	Clare Farm/PowersPlace
Smith, William M	1919	Clare Farm/PowersPlace
Smith, William M	1923	Clare Farm/PowersPlace
Smith, William M	1899	Clifton/Meadors
Smith, William M	1908	Effingham House
Smith, William M	1917	Jiltic Farm/Booker's Mill
Smith, William M	1919	Willow Bank/Isbell
Smith, William R & L L	before 1902	Bookers Tavern

Owner	Year	Subject
Smith, William Robert	1895	Locust Grove/Flippen
Smith, Wm W	1911	Solitude
Snead, Dr N P	1897	White Level
Snyder, Mrs Sallie	1937	Hickory Hall
Southall, Cary	1816	Southall
Southall, John	1778	Southall
Southall, Walter C	1873	Scott Home/Flippen Home
Spencer, A S	1912	Clay Bank
Spencer, D H D - 1812-1844		Mountain View/Locust Level - inscription
Spencer, Elizabeth W	1844	Mountain View/Locust Level
Spencer, Elizabeth W - 1793-1850		Mountain View/Locust Level - inscription
Spencer, John	1839	Mountain View/Locust Level
Spencer, John - 1786-1845		Mountain View/Locust Level - inscription
Spencer, John D - 1810-1844		Mountain View/Locust Level - inscription
Spencer, Lion G	1839	Mountain View/Locust Level
Spencer, Sidney Bruce	1993	Corson Home/Coupland's Tavern
Spencer, W S	1916	Clay Bank
Spencer, William V - 1820-1858		Mountain View/Locust Level - inscription
Steger, Ann E (Bradley)	1881	Rock Spring
Steger, Francis E H	after 1839	Broomfield/Steger's Farm
Steger, Nancy	1839	Broomfield/Steger's Farm
Steger, Thomas H	1796	Broomfield/Steger's Farm
Stevens, Absolem	1855	Gravel Hill
Stibbins, Joseph Jr	1913	Millview
Stiger, Francis E P - trustee	1856	Fork of Willis Church
Stout, Charles A	1910	Woodlawn/Cooper
Stout, Walter C	1910	Woodlawn/Cooper
Stover, Mr & Mrs Wm C	1926	Willow Bank/Isbell
Stratton, Milton M	1901	Cedar Grove/Bryant Place
Stratton, William	1845	Refuge
Stuart, Charlotte - heirs		Spring Hill/Cook's Tract

Owner	Year	Subject
Stuart, Charlotte (Mrs D Henry)	1875	Spring Hill/Cook's Tract
Stuart, David		Spring Hill/Cook's Tract
Stuart, F H	1910	Spring Hill/Cook's Tract
Stuart, Walter	1904	Overton Home (Old)
Sutphin, James	1831	Rock Spring
Sutton, Mrs Hallie (Shores)	1930	Glentivar
Swann, J Singleton - heirs	1938	Popepand/Swann Place
Swann, James Singleton	1886	Popepand/Swann Place
Swann, Sallie	1797	Popepand/Swann Place
Swann, Sallie - heirs		Popepand/Swann Place
Swift, Mr & Mrs	1936	Bizarre
Tabb, John	before 1778	Southall
Taliaferro, M W	1883	Rochelle
Talley, Abner	1929	Refuge
Talley, Ann D	1906	Refuge
Talley, Dr Zack - trustee	1846	Thomas Chapel
Talley, Edwin P	1852	Auburn
Talley, Edwin P	1851	Palmer's Tavern
Talley, Jack	1815	Talley Home
Talley, James Madison - 1793		Glebe, The - inscription
Talley, Nelson - heirs	before 1908	Talley Home
Talley, William C	1852	Morven
Talley, Zach	before 1852	Reynolds Home
Taylor, Annie & Emily		Needham
Taylor, Creed	1787	Needham
Taylor, Creed	1853	Needham
Taylor, Creed		Needham - burial
Taylor, Creed & Samuel	1843	Needham
Taylor, Emily	1916	Needham
Taylor, John D	1812	Felixville
Taylor, Mrs Creed	1832	Needham
Taylor, Samuel	1823	Hors du Monde
Taylor, Samuel	before 1787	Needham
Taylor, Samuel	before 1760	Refuge
Taylor, William	1814	Felixville
Terrell, A J	1912	Mount Elba
Thackston, Elizabeth Rosa	1860	Thackston Home (Old)
Thackston, John	1843	Peabody Place (Old)
Thackston, Richard D		Thackston Home (Old)
Theimer, Mary - Mrs Frank	1872	Scott Home/Flippen Home

Owner	Year	Subject
Thomas, James		Gravel Hill
Thomas, Jesse	before 1776	Jesse Thomas Site
Thomas, Joseph	before 1835	Gravel Hill
Thompson, Benjamin		Foster Place (Old)/Hobson Place
Thompson, Josiah	1778	Langhorne's Tavern
Thompson, William		Langhorne's Tavern
Thorbus, C T	1906	Clare Farm/PowersPlace
Thornton, Capt William	before 1856	Oak Hill
Thornton, Charles Irving - 1841-1842		Oak Hill Cemetery - inscription
Thornton, John T	1856	Oak Hill
Thornton, Mary W		Oak Hill
Thornton, Richard C	1856	Oak Hill
Thornton, William M	1806	Ca Ira Mill
Thrawn, Carl	1906	Clare Farm/PowersPlace
Thurston, T J & C L	1901	Mount Elba
Thweatt, Archibald	before 1810	Cherry Grove/Thweatt
Toff, Fred W	1909	Overton Home (Old)
Toler, Miller	1874	Mount Airy
Toler, Minnie	1874	Mount Airy
Toler, Sarah M - legatee	before 1852	Rose Cottage
Toler, William & Frances	before 1852	Mount Airy
Toler, William B	1874	Mount Airy
Toler, William B & Miller H		Rose Cottage
Toler, William E & Samuel	by 1936	Rose Cottage
Toler, William L	1852	Mount Airy
Toler, William L - legatee	before 1852	Rose Cottage
Treakle, A F	1913	Spring Hill/Cook's Tract
Trent, Albert	by 1936	Colwell Graveyard
Trent, Albert	by 1936	Glebe, The
Trent, Alexander	1790	Trenton Mill/Sport's Lake
Trent, Alexander	1816	Farmview
Trent, Alexander	1850	Springfield
Trent, Alexander (1703-1751)	1735	Barter Hill
Trent, Alexander (1729-1793)	ca 1751	Barter Hill
Trent, Alexander (1729-1793)	before 1790	Auburn
Trent, Alexander - vestryman	1772	Glebe, The - Church of England
Trent, Alexander (1758-1804)	1789	Barter Hill
Trent, Alexander (1758-1804)	after 1767	Trent's Mill

Owner	Year	Subject
Trent, Alexander Jr	1823	Farmview
Trent, Alexander (1786-1873)	1823	Clay Bank
Trent Alexander V (1786-1873)		Clay Bank - graveyard
Trent, Dr John (1789-1862)	about 1825	Trenton/Brick House
Trent, Edward	before 1816	Farmview
Trent, Elizabeth Randolph (1803-1882)		Clay Bank - graveyard
Trent, Isaiah	1883	Woodside Site
Trent, J A & A L	1903	Trenton/Brick House
Trent, John	1816	Stony Point/Stony Mill Site
Trent, John A	1794	Trenton Mill/Sport's Lake
Trent, John L	1841	Trenton Mill/Sport's Lake
Trent, Mary Anne	ca 1804	Trent's Mill
Trent, Mary B - 1815-1856		Trenton - inscription
Trent, Peterfield		Trenton Mill/Sport's Lake
Trent, Stephen W	1843	Trent's Mill
Trent, Stephen W	1918	Union Hill
Trent, Stephen W m Eliz. B Coupland	1794	Springfield
Trent, Stephen Woodson	1790	Auburn
Trent, W J	1903	Trenton/Brick House
Trent, William A	1838	Trent's Mill
Trent, William A	1843	Trent's Mill
Trent, William A - trustee	1847	Center Presbyterian Church
Trevillian, John M	1845	Hooper's Rock
Trice, Benjamin	by 1936	Walton's Mill
Trice, P J	1900	Gravel Hill
Trice, P J	1890	Oakland/Carrington
Trice, Phillip I	1893	Walton's Mill
Trigg, William - Tavern-Keeper	1747	Effingham House
Tuggle, Thomas T	before 1824	Guinea Church/Tuggle's Meeting House
Tyree, David - trustee	1811	Felixville
Tyson, A L	after 1936	Cedar Grove/Bryant Place
Upchurch, Mrs Lillie		Bookers Tavern
Venable, Abraham B	before 1791	Bonbrook
Waits, Mary	1917	Reynolds Home
Walden, John E	1855	Cherry Grove/Sanderson Home
Walker, C M	1896	Dunleith
Walker, David & Elizabeth		Woodlawn/Epps
Walker, E S	1889	Locust Grove Cemetery

Owner	Year	Subject
Walker, E S	1889	Locust Grove/Nelson
Walker, Elizabeth (Epps)	1800	Woodlawn/Epps
Walker, Ellen M - heirs		White Hall/Walker Place/Cemetery
Walker, H S & W D	1929	White Hall/Walker Place/Cemetery
Walker, John E - 1888-1906		Locust Grove Cemetery - inscription
Walker, Sallie - 1867-1900		Locust Grove Cemetery - inscription
Walker, Warren	1752	White Hall/Walker Place/Cemetery
Walker, William	before 1838	Peaceful Level
Walker, William	before 1752	White Hall/Walker Place/Cemetery
Walker, William	1785	White Hall/Walker Place/Cemetery
Walker, William B B	1828	White Hall/Walker Place/Cemetery
Walker, William D	1870	White Hall/Walker Place/Cemetery
Walker, William D - widow	1879	White Hall/Walker Place/Cemetery
Wall, J B	1899	Overton Home (Old)
Wallace, Sam	1814	Felixville
Wallace, William	1814	Felixville
Walthall, Henry C & Mary (Hughes)	by 1937	Peaceful Level
Walton, Anthony A	1850	Englewood/Horn Quarter
Walton, Dr Richard (1819-1898)	1857	Morningside
Walton, Frances Ann (Carrington)	ca 1808	Walton's Mill
Walton, Nathaniel - trustee	1846	Thomas Chapel
Walton, Thomas H	1830	Walton's Mill
Warren, Howell E	1857	Thackston Home (Old)
Watkins, Bennett	1879	Midway/Langhorne's Home
Watkins, Richard	1834	Langhorne's Tavern
Watkins, Richard	1834	Midway/Langhorne's Home
Watkins, Richard V & Polly	1859	Woodlawn/Ross
Watson	before 1992	Somerset Site

Owner	Year	Subject
Watson, Ray	before 1992	Bonbrook
Watson, Ray	before 1992	Bonbrook Cemetery
Wharey, Mary Blanton		Oak Grove
Whisnant, Lena	1936	Peabody Place (Old)
Whitehead, F A	1876	Woodville Site
Whitehead, I P & wife	1876	Woodville Site
Whitlock, George	before 1993	Morven
Whitlock, Jennie (Brazeal)	before 1932	Frayser's Tavern
Wiley, John - trustee	1811	Felixville
Wilkinson family		Wilkinson Cemetery
Wilkinson, B S - -1860		Wilkinson Cemetery - inscription
Wilkinson, D - -1860		Wilkinson Cemetery - inscription
Wilkinson, Ducalion	1855	Trenton Mill/Sport's Lake
Wilkinson, Essie B & others	1899	Rosebank
Wilkinson, George T	1880	Trenton Mill/Sport's Lake
Wilkinson, George T	1903	Trenton Mill/Sport's Lake
Wilkinson, Jane	1860	Trenton Mill/Sport's Lake
Wilkinson, R H - -1872		Wilkinson Cemetery - inscription
Wilson, Albert	1883	Glebe, The
Wilson, Allen	before 1827	Spring Hill/Cook's Tract
Wilson, Allen & wife	before 1843	Woodville Site
Wilson, Allen (1780-1849)	ca 1827	Underhill Site
Wilson, Benjamin - vestryman	1772	Glebe, The - Church of England
Wilson, Benjamin (1733-1814)	1755	Somerset Site
Wilson, Benjamin, Matthew & Goodrich	1842	Somerset Site
Wilson, Benjamin, Matthew & Goodrich	1847	Somerset Site
Wilson, Daniel A	1819	Cherry Grove/Thweatt
Wilson, Dr Samuel (1770-1841)	1815	Somerset Site
Wilson, Edward	1852-1877	Somerset Site
Wilson, Edward		Trent's Mill
Wilson, Edward - 1819-1893		Barter Hill - inscription
Wilson, Elizabeth - 1785-1851		Barter Hill - inscription
Wilson, Elizabeth (Trent) & children	1834	Barter Hill

Owner   Year   Subject

Wilson, Elizabeth Woodson (Trent)
- 1807-1888   Bonbrook Cemetery -
                                                 inscription
Wilson, Fanny P   1880   Cedar Bluff/Scott Place
Wilson, Goodrich   1853   Barter Hill
Wilson, Henry J - 1848-1884   Bonbrook Cemetery -
                                                 inscription
Wilson, Henry J & wife Lucy 1879   Bonbrook
Wilson, Isaac Gibson - 1863-1864   Bonbrook Cemetery -
                                                 inscription
Wilson, James   1796 & 1798   Clay Bank
Wilson, James   1816   Barter Hill
Wilson, James   1823   Farmview
Wilson, John P   1843   Trent's Mill
Wilson, John P - trustee   1847   Center Presbyterian Church
Wilson, John Park - 1790-1871   Bonbrook Cemetery -
                                                 inscription
Wilson, John R   1869   Buena Vista Site
Wilson, John R   1848   Midway/Langhorne's Home
Wilson, John W   1869   Buena Vista Site
Wilson, John W   1870   High Hill
Wilson, John W   1827   Spring Hill/Cook's Tract
Wilson, John W - daughters   1870   Hors du Monde
Wilson, John W - heirs   1875   Spring Hill/Cook's Tract
Wilson, John W & wife   before 1843   Woodville Site
Wilson, John W (ca 1796-1870) before 1870   Hors du Monde
Wilson, Junius L   1888   Overton Home (Old)
Wilson, Maria Willis (Wilson)
- 1793-1818   Bonbrook Cemetery -
                                                 inscription
Wilson, Martha J - 1835-1860   Locust Grove Cemetery -
                                                 inscription

Wilson, Matthew
& Elizabeth (Trent)   ca 1809   Barter Hill
Wilson, Mrs Lucy (Gay)
& Miss Bettie C Gay   1887   Bonbrook
Wilson, Richard (1752-1827) ca 1807   Underhill Site
Wilson, Samuel (1811-1886)   before 1849   Viewmont
Wilson, Thomas Friend   1857   Woodlawn/Epps
Wilson, William W   1847   Bonbrook
Wilson, William W   1845   Trent's Mill

Owner	Year	Subject
Wilson, William W - trustee	1847	Center Presbyterian Church
Wilson, William W & Willis	1823	Bonbrook
Wilson, Willis	1791	Bonbrook
Wilson, Willis - 1758-1822		Bonbrook Cemetery - inscription
Wilson, Willis Park - 1815-1816		Bonbrook Cemetery - inscription
Wilson, Willis, James, Goodrich - exrs.	1815	Somerset Site
Winifree, H Lee	1912	Scott Home/Flippen Home
Winifree, W R	1903	Melrose
Winston, William Henry	1911	Solitude
Wisdom, Craddock	before 1837	Boston Hill
Wisdom, C died July 12, 1837		Boston Hill - inscription
Womack, Charles	before 1811	Womack Place (Old)
Womack, Charles	1899	Woodville Site
Womack, Mary	1937	Hickory Hall
Womack, Nathan	1856	Hickory Hall
Womack, Nathan	1875	Hors du Monde
Womack, Nathan	1925	Woodlawn/Epps
Womack, Nathan - widow & children	1903	Hors du Monde
Womack, Pattie C	1925	Hickory Hall
Wood, Cabell S	before 1907	Stony Point/Stony Mill Site
Wood, Dr Richard	1889	Stony Point/Stony Mill Site
Wood, John Phillip	1920	Clare Farm/PowersPlace
Wood, John T	1857	Glentivar
Wood, John T	1853	Pleasant Grove
Wood, John T	1856	Walton's Mill
Wood, Joshua R	1909	Gravel Hill
Wood, Warrington	before 1907	Stony Point/Stony Mill Site
Wood, Watson		Glentivar
Woodfin, Elisha Sr	1849	Ashland
Woodfin, Sarah	1855	Ashland
Woodson, Alexander, Tscharner & Miller Jr	1823	Glebe, The
Woodson, Ann S - 1777-1826		Deanery Cemetery - inscription
Woodson, B B	1871	Ca Ira Mill
Woodson, B B	1906	Clare Farm/PowersPlace
Woodson, B B	1908	Effingham House

Owner	Year	Subject
Woodson, B B	1911	Hickory Hill/Hard Bargain
Woodson, B B	1910	Mill Mount
Woodson, B B	1911	Solitude
Woodson, B B	1870	Willow Bank/Isbell
Woodson, Blake B	1880	Mill Mount
Woodson, Charles	1796	Rocky Mount
Woodson, Charles	Before 1788	Rosebank
Woodson, H D	1910	Mill Mount
Woodson, James B	1816	Stony Point/Stony Mill Site
Woodson, Jessie	1804	Rocky Mount
Woodson, John - 1716-1793		Deanery Cemetery - inscription
Woodson, John - 1765-1832		Deanery Cemetery - inscription
Woodson, John M	ca 1832	Rochelle
Woodson, John P - 1795-1815		Deanery Cemetery - inscription
Woodson, Miller	before 1823	Glebe, The
Woodson, Mrs Lillie P	1925	Mill Mount
Woodson, Tarleton	ca 1830	Rosebank
Woodson, Tarleton - trustee	1846	Thomas Chapel
Woodson, William	ca 1830	Rosebank
Word, Thomas - Tavern-Keeper	1760	Effingham House
Wright, George	before 1783	Raines Tavern/Wright's Ordinary
Wright, George - vestryman	1772	Glebe, The - Church of England
Wright, Henry	1783	Raines Tavern/Wright's Ordinary
Yancy, John	1814	Corson Home/Coupland's Tavern
Yancy, John		Rose Hill
Yancy, Robert	1814	Corson Home/Coupland's Tavern
Zimmerman, C E	1921	Blanton Home (Old)
Zimmerman, Harry M		Pleasant Grove

Bibliography

Avant, David A. *Some Southern Colonial Families*. 4 vols. Tallahassee FL: L'Avant Studios, 1983-91.

Brandow, James C. "The Origin of the Carrington Family in Virginia". *National Genealogical Society Quarterly* 70 (1982):246-270.

Brown, Alexander. *The Cabells and Their Kin*. Franklin, NC: Genealogy Pub. Service, 1994.

Brown, Elizabeth Trent Wight. *Genealogical notes concerning the Wight and Wilson families*. Mss 6:1 W6395:2. Virginia Historical Society, Richmond. This contains "Family Record" written by Elizabeth Woodson Trent in 1876.

Carlton, Nannie Page Trent. "Brief History of the Trent Family of Cumberland County, Virginia." B. S., Longwood College, 1938.

Cox, Julia Bransford and James R Cox. *Works Progress Administration Historical Inventory of Cumberland County (Alphabetical index by subject)*. 1996.

Crawford, Alan Pell. *Unwise Passions, A True Story of a Remarkable Woman - and the First Great Scandal of Eighteenth-Century America*. New York: Simon & Schuster, 2000.

Cumberland County Virginia Historical Bulletin. Cumberland VA: The Cumberland County Historical Society.

Cumberland County Virginia and Its People. Cumberland VA: Cumberland County Historical Society, 1983.

Dorman, John Frederick, ed., comp. *Adventurers of Purse and Person Virginia 1607-1624/25*. 4th edition. Baltimore: Genealogical Publishing Co, 2004.

Elliott, Katherine B., comp. *Marriage Records 1749-1840, Cumberland County Virginia*. 1969. Reprint, Easley SC: Southern Historical Press, 1983.

Genealogies of Virginia Families from The Virginia Magazine of History and Biography. 5 vols. Baltimore: Genealogical Publishing Co, 1981.

Gish, Dr Agnes E. "Effingham Tavern". *Cumberland County, Virginia Historical Bulletin* 13(1988):13-14. Cumberland VA: Cumberland County Historical Society.

"Graveyards and Markers in Cumberland County". *Cumberland County, Virginia Historical Bulletin* 1(1984):40-1. Cumberland VA: Cumberland County Historical Society.

Littleton Parish (Cumberland County, Va.). *Records, 1840-1899*. Accession 29330, Church Records Collection, Library of Virginia, Richmond.

McCrary, Patti Sue. *Wilson Families in Cumberland County Virginia and Woodford County Kentucky with Correspondence and Other Papers 1785-1849*. Westminster, MD: Willow Bend Books, 2005.

McIlwaine, H R, ed. *Proceedings of the Committees of Safety of Cumberland and Isle of Wight Counties Virginia 1775-1776*. Richmond: Davis Bottom, Superintendent of Public Printing, 1919.

"Notes from Cumberland County Court Order Book (No. 2) 1752-1758," *Sharpe in Virginia*, Vol. 1, No. 1 (1 Oct 2000), (www.thecolonist.com).

Notes on Peter Field Trent. Microfiche 6019060. Family History Library, Salt Lake City, Utah.

Putney, Dorothy Rhodes. "Tar Wallet Baptist Church". Vertical File, Cumberland County Public Library. Cumberland VA: 1993.

Reynolds, Katherine, abs. *Abstracts of Cumberland County, Virginia, Will Books 1 and 2 1749-1782*. Easley, SC: Southern Historical Press, 1985.

Robins, Mrs A S. "Goshen". *Cumberland County, Virginia Historical Bulletin* 1 (1984):35. Cumberland VA: Cumberland County Historical Society.

Stanard, W G. "Harrison of James River". *Genealogies of Virginia Families from The Virginia Magazine of History and Biography* 3(1922-1932):687-844. Baltimore: Genealogical Publishing Co, 1981.

Stanley, Mildred M. "Guinea Presbyterian Church". *Cumberland County,*

Virginia Historical Bulletin (1(1984):30-1. Cumberland VA: Cumberland County Historical Society.

Stockman, Mrs Sadie. "Glentivar". *Cumberland County, Virginia Historical Bulletin* 2 (1985):43. Cumberland VA: Cumberland County Historical Society.

Stutesman, John Hale. *Some Watkins Families of Virginia and their Kin*. Baltimore: Gateway Press, 1989.

Swinson, Sherry. "Rochelle". *Cumberland County, Virginia Historical Bulletin* 12(1997):14-15. Cumberland VA: Cumberland County Historical Society.

Today and Yesterday in the Heart of Virginia. Farmville VA: Farmville Herald, 1935.

Vaughan, M K. *Crucible and Cornerstone – A History of Cumberland County, Virginia*. Atlanta: Resource Development Internship Project, 1969.

Wall, Jackie. "Forlorn Remains of Famed Patriot and Family". *Cumberland County, Virginia Historical Bulletin* 12(1997):8-9. Cumberland VA: Cumberland County Historical Society.

Watkins, Marie Oliver and Helen (Hamacher) Watkins. *Tearin' Through the Wilderness: Missouri Pioneer Episodes, 1822-1885, and Genealogy of the Watkins Family of Virginia and Missouri*. Charleston WV: Mathews Printing, 1957.

Weisiger, Benjamin B III, comp. *Goochland County, Virginia, Wills and Deeds, 1728-1736*. [Richmond, Va.] : Weisiger, c1983.

Will of Benjamin Wilson, 1812-1814. Cumberland County VA Lodged Wills, Box 1, The Library of Virginia, Richmond.

Wilson, Cornelia Williamson McLaurine, comp. *Genealogical notes on the Harris, McLaurine, St. Clair, Stegar, Williamson, and Wilson families*. Mss6:1 W691:1. Virginia Historical Society, Richmond.

Wilson, Cornelia McLaurine, Family History, transcribed by Philip Austin Lawless of Durham NC.
ftp://ftp.rootsweb.com/pub/usgenweb/tx/sanaugustine/history/w4250001.txt

Woodson, Henry Morton, comp. *Historical Genealogy of the Woodsons and Their Connections.* [Memphis] the author, 1915.

CPSIA information can be obtained at www.ICGtesting.com
Printed in the USA
LVOW05s1203290713

345161LV00021B/833/P